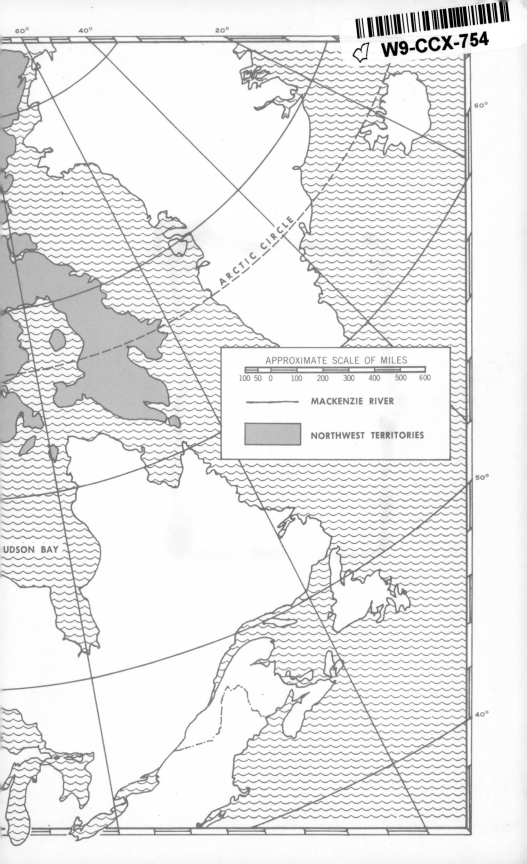

60°   40°   20°

60°

ARCTIC CIRCLE

APPROXIMATE SCALE OF MILES

100 50 0   100   200   300   400   500   600

———— MACKENZIE RIVER

NORTHWEST TERRITORIES

50°

UDSON BAY

40°

EX LIBRIS

JONES COLLECTION

KAYAKS TO THE ARCTIC

Kayaks to the Arctic

E. B. NICKERSON

Photographs by Richard A. Nickerson

Howell-North Books • Berkeley, California • 1967

KAYAKS TO THE ARCTIC

Printed and bound in the United States of America
Library of Congress Catalog Card No. 67-27369

Second Printing, June, 1970

ISBN 0-8310-7065-X

Published by Howell-North Books
1050 Parker Street, Berkeley, California 94710

CONTENTS

For my parents
FRIEDA AND JAMES BARKLEY

I «
THE MIGHTY MACKENZIE

Most silver wedding anniversaries call for something special: a second honeymoon in Bermuda or the Islands; a mink coat or a sable stole. For our twenty-fifth year my husband took me to the Arctic, one thousand miles in a kayak; and I came home wearing duffel mukluks and a rat parka.

Three of our sons were with us too: Devon, age 19, a college junior; Lincoln, a seventh grader who turned 12 on the trip; and Brian, 10 years old, sixth grade. These boys have been camping since before they could walk. Brian was three when we turned in our packsacks for kayaks and traded our hiking shoes for double-bladed paddles. We are all hardy, seasoned, experienced campers. But nothing could have prepared us for the sheer magic of the mighty Mackenzie.

This river rises full grown at a width of more than two miles from the Great Slave Lake, far up in Canada's Northwest Territories and empties into the Beaufort Sea of the Arctic Ocean some 1100 miles away. The little community of Fort Providence marks its real beginning, and the settlements all along its course carry names brimming with excitement: Jean Marie Creek, Fort Simpson, Fort Wrigley, Fort Norman, Norman Wells, Fort Good Hope, Arctic Red River, Aklavik, Reindeer Station, Inuvik, Tuktoyaktuk. Freeze-up begins at the mouth of the river in September, and break-up does not reach Tuk until late June; but for those brief weeks between we found soft summer air, swift water, good companions, and complete escape from the thralldom of telephone, radio, and TV. We also found mosquitoes, and blackflies, and bulldog flies (whatever they really are, I don't know. That's what the natives call them), and storms, rapids, bears, fish. . . . And people—wonderful, friendly people who made us welcome in many different ways.

I remember a fresh baked loaf of bread on the beach of a tiny Indian village; the campsite on the front lawn of a Grey Nun's Hospital; a cocktail party without peer or parallel even in San Francisco; breakfast in a construction camp mess hall; tea and bannock at a fish camp in the Delta; friendship and shelter with an Eskimo. Then there were the people of the tug-boats and barges who always were on the lookout for us. Royal Canadian Mounted Police offered campsites and docks guaranteed to keep our belongings safe; and they monitored our arrivals and departures between towns, ready to send searchers if we dropped far behind schedule. Indians in canoes, scows, speedboats, all driven by powerful modern "kickers," waved at us, sometimes stopped and shared our coffee and their fish, and passed the word through the moccasin telegraph: "The Kayaking Family is safe and well, and will be along soon."

But the distance from the San Francisco International Airport to the gravel landing strip at Yellowknife covered far more than the 2500 miles we actually flew and spread over in point of time four decades of my life.

When I was a little girl my family went camping every summer. This was in the 1920's. We set up base camp in Yosemite and spent the greater part of our vacation hiking. As I grew older I went to Girl Scout Camp and although we did some hiking there, the best times of all were the canoe trip overnights. The summer before I married I was a counselor in the St. Paul, Minnesota, Girl Scout Camp where five-day canoe trips on the St. Croix River were the highlight of the whole camp program. It seemed to me then, as it does now, that drifting down a river in a motorless craft is just about the best method in the world of "getting away from it all."

Meanwhile my husband-to-be grew up in a family that "camped" in hotels, such as the Coronado on San Diego's Silver Strand, or the Lodge at the Oregon Caves. I think he had his first camp-out on an army bivouac during World War II, an experience which hardly could be said to count. After the war we tried a two-week back-packing fishing trip together, and he found out that neither the Coronado nor the Army were ever like this. The children came along, and back packing evolved into mule and horseback trips. Then one summer, while staying at a mountain lake, we rented kayaks for an afternoon and we were hooked.

Now we own three of them, touring models, and a whole new world has been opened up to us. Unlike canoes, kayaks ride low in the water, and are difficult to capsize. Paddling requires little skill for there is no need to trade a single blade from side to side, or "drag" or "J-stroke" to keep them on course. Best of all they can be taken apart, stuffed into canvas containers, and shipped anywhere.

We made our first real trip for 75 miles on the Willamette River in Oregon. When our youngest son was 5 we toured the 120 miles of the Glen Canyon of the Colorado, the year before the dam turned it into Lake Powell. Three years later we traveled from White Horse to Dawson City on the Yukon. Each of these unguided tours seems now like a lead-up to the Mackenzie River.

We heard about the Mackenzie when we returned from the Yukon. A reporter from a San Francisco newspaper told us about the river after an interview about the White Horse-Dawson City trip. His name is Luther Duc Meyer (we call him Duc and pronounce it Duke), and he will appear more prominently in this book by and by. So, for our silver anniversary we headed north.

Incidentally, the mukluks are Indian, from Fort Franklin, N.W.T., so beautifully beaded that they were on exhibit at the Canadian Women's Institute Convention, held this year at Inuvik, where I bought them. My "rat" parka is "muskrat," called "rat" in the Arctic. It is trimmed in silky wolverine. It was made by an Eskimo craftsman in the fur co-op at Aklavik. It is beautiful, and I wear it proudly.

2 «

YELLOWKNIFE

We decided to fly from the Bay Area to Yellowknife, then take the bus around the Great Slave Lake through Fort Rae to Fort Providence. There we would assemble our kayaks and put in the river for "the real part of the vacation" as Brian, our youngest, called it, but having made this decision we then had to arrange for shipping our equipment.

When completely packed, there were 24 pieces of baggage as follows:

5 knapsacks with clothes and sleeping bags
1 duffel bag of life jackets
1 duffel bag of tents
1 package of guns and fishing tackle
1 canvas bag of cooking equipment
2 large cartons of dried and dehydrated food
2 waterproof boxes containing more food
8 canvas bags with the parts of three folding kayaks, including 5 sets of paddles
3 cases of film

Of course our first thought was to carry as much as we could on our tickets, but we learned a few things about passenger airlines when it came to arranging for the excess baggage. Their thinking centers on passengers each carrying "two pieces of hand luggage" and beyond this they are well-meaning but not helpful. Their advice to bring along the extra pieces at plane time was so unrealistic (the total weight was approximately nine hundred pounds) that it could not be followed, so we spent a lot of time arranging their transport by air freight from Oakland to Yellowknife ten days in advance of our flight from San Francisco for a charge of one hundred and eighty dollars.

Tuesday morning, June 21, at 5:00 a.m. I was glad to be awake although I hate early rising. What a night before we'd had! Company for dinner, then people dropping by to hoist a stirrup cup, and last-minute phone calls to wish us well. The family turned in at 11:00, with me promising to follow quickly. Two and a half hours later I finished writing the last check and the final instructions for our eldest son, Steven, who would stay home in charge of the house. Five o'clock was welcome. Who could sleep?

By six we were all ready and had a light snack. Our traveling clothes were simple since we planned no touring side trips. Nick and Devon and the boys wore new jeans, turtle-neck shirts, tennis shoes and sweatshirts. I was more formally dressed in black capris, white blouse, gold Italian knit sweater and black ankle-height boots. The station wagon was packed the night before, so all we had to do was climb in and be off, missing the commuter traffic which clogs the freeways by 7:00, and breakfasting leisurely at the airport some time around 7:30. Our plane left at 9:00.

My husband is a metallurgical engineer at Lawrence Radiation Laboratory. He is tall, slender, grey haired, mustached, wears glasses, and is generally quiet and soft spoken. This image was temporarily shattered when, airport-bound, we walked out to the garage and found the right rear tire flat!

After this annoying delay, and the seemingly endless trip across the San Francisco-Oakland Bay Bridge and down the Peninsula, we finally arrived at the San Francisco airport. Our knapsacks and fishing tackle and guns and boxes collected a gratifying number of stares, not to mention our own selves, burdened as we were with camera cases and film cans.

"Suppose we'd shown up with nine hundred pounds of excess baggage," I whispered to Nick as we checked through the long ticket line.

"What a flap!" he chuckled.

We felt smug looking at the common travelers and boarded our plane in time, albeit with empty stomachs.

Not much can be said for a three-hour stopover in Vancouver: too long to clear customs, too short to get out of the airport. But at 4:15 that afternoon we were in Edmonton with a twenty-hour layover ahead, and soon were riding the airport bus to town.

I was a little worried about where we were going to stay overnight. Back home I earnestly told the travel agency: "What we really want is a nice little family hotel — one that a businessman not on an expense account might use; not fancy, but clean and loving children."

Our agent consulted a couple of airline pilots and learned that our flight took us into the International Airport, but that we left from the Industrial Airport which is practically downtown. She booked rooms at "an old established hotel" just about fourteen blocks from the Industrial Airport.

In due course we drove up to this old established hotel — the Macdonald. This is the direct equivalent of being dropped at the front entrance of San Francisco's Mark Hopkins, St. Francis or Sheraton-Palace.

Lincoln immediately shot out of the limousine, dashed up the stairs, and disappeared in the revolving door.

"Devon, get him!" I hissed. Devon took off.

"I'll find him," Brian called helpfully, dodging my grasp, and raced off too.

The doorman stared at us.

Tableau!

"Good afternoon," said Nick.

I started to count baggage.

The man smiled.

"Welcome to Edmonton," he said, and signaled the bell captain. The captain beckoned a boy, and the boy came out with a large canvas cart in which our ten pieces of camping gear were soon stowed. The three brothers, having been reunited in the men's room, were waiting quietly for us in the lobby.

There must have been a dozen or more well-dressed businessmen in somber charcoal suits near the desk. I could feel their interested and, I suppose, amused looks. But I did not have long to think about them for a young reporter came forward to interview us. Little did we dream that twelve hundred miles later one of these men would be our host. The reporter, the family and the baggage all went upstairs to our simple two-room, two-bath, two-TV suite.

Lincoln could hardly contain himself.

"A TV in each room! I'm going to watch them both at once," he exclaimed.

"Start with the one in your room," Nick advised. "We're busy just now."

Linc is the true primitive of our family. In appearance he is beguiling, with clear blue eyes, golden blonde hair, rosy complexion, and dimples. He moves with all the coordination and energy of the born athlete; he is a dynamo, constantly on the go, continually into everything. He wants to know how and where and why, asks the most searching questions, tests and experiments for himself whenever he can. The miracle of flight has always fascinated him, and on this trip he was to be introduced to two things: unlimited bird watching and the intriguing life of the bush pilot. We knew that once we were out of the big cities Linc would be in his element, but until then we had to keep him dampered down.

Brian, on the other hand, has a more civilized approach to life. His personality is winsome, his disposition thoughtful and amiable. He is tall for his age, stocky of build, with brown hair, grey-green eyes, and the memory of an elephant. While Linc burbled about the television Brian quietly inspected the plumbing.

He reported, "There's a great big bathtub on a platform in your bathroom. I hope this hotel has a large enough water heater!"

This was an oblique reference to the cold shower he had had to take in a Dawson City hotel in the Yukon three years ago; he has never trusted hotel hot water supplies since.

We shooed Brian into the other room to watch TV and Devon and Nick and I turned to the novel business of being interviewed by a real live reporter. It was fun.

No sooner had we exchanged introductions than we found a mutual friend; the reporter had roomed across the hall in college from the son of the PTA president with whom I had served as second vice president in 1963. Do you follow me? (Small world!) But Geron Summers, cub though he may have been, conducted a workmanlike, interesting, painless interview, and had a nice article published in the Edmonton *Journal* the next morning. We parted cordially and started for dinner.

In some deference to propriety we decided that we simply could not have dinner in the hotel dining room dressed as we were. We left the Macdonald to see what we could find in the line of a short-order eatery and soon saw what we thought was just right: nondescript store front, plain red paint on white sign with a temporary "being remodeled-business-as-usual" look. The name: Steak Loft. We walked in the door and were confronted not by a steamy, smoky lunchroom counter, but by a flight of stairs. A shrug or two later we had climbed to the top, turned a corner, and entered a carpeted loggia complete with check-girl, reservation desk, green growing plants, and black-tied maître d'hôtel.

Ignoring the egg on our faces we allowed ourselves to be led to a table while, again, I could feel the quizzical looks of the earlier dinner guests peering at us from behind three-foot menus and over small table candles. Brian and Linc were so "awed up" by the sheer swank of this lovely little restaurant that they moved to their places in subdued and proper fashion. Devon seemed to be having a little trouble suppressing his emotions. (Whether it was a compulsion to giggle or to panic I never learned.) By imagining I was wearing my basic black, I found it fairly easy to let myself be seated.

Nick ordered grenadines for the boys and Harvey's Bristol Cream sherry for us, glanced briefly at the menu and requested steaks, salad, and the wine list. Another glance and he had summoned a fifth of Pommard. The water boy paused, the wine steward smiled, the waiter bowed slightly, and the maitre de, passing by on another errand, asked us how we liked Canada. Soon the chef appeared to confirm the cut of beef and invite the younger boys to watch their meat being grilled.

By the time our dinner ended, almost the entire restaurant staff had heard of our trip to come. They told us to be sure to dine with them on our return even though our plane was due in at midnight for the Steak Loft was open until 2:00 a.m. All down the river we remembered that delicious meal and the incomparable hospitality. Even now Linc speaks wistfully of the salad dressing.

Unfortunately, our return plane was three hours late, so we never saw them again.

In the morning we did something I had always wanted to do but had never done before: ordered breakfast sent up to our rooms. Such a great amount of napery and silver, underliners and warmers, crockery and glassware, and food! We relished every bit, telling ourselves life would soon be different. Two mornings later we were to remember that breakfast as we sat on the floor of our tent and stared out at the mosquito-blackened screen door.

We flew to Yellowknife, arriving in the afternoon. Our bus to Fort Providence left at midnight. We had seven hours and were looking forward to browsing and shopping for at least part of the evening, but alas, in the Northwest Territories, Wednesday is early-closing day, so we never saw the inside of a single store. But we got a good look at the town, and it is a most interesting place. There is a waterfront for river craft of all kinds, including huge barges and powerful tugs which run the length of the Mackenzie waterway. There is a snye for float-planes as well as the larger airport two miles from town. The city itself has an old town and a new town, the former with log structures here and there that date back more than fifty years, and one main street runs from new town on the hill to old town by the water. The mosquito concentration increases in direct proportion to the descent to the bottom of the hill. Sidewalks, too, change from concrete to board to nonexistent as you approach old town. But these things are as they should be. We were at Yellowknife only long enough to get a quick impression and to leave feeling it was a place we would like to visit again.

After dinner we went to the movie, a Terry Thomas comedy. The theater auditorium had an unusually steep slant, soft drinks were sold in bottles, and the empties were deftly sent rolling and booted along from feet to feet till they reached the bottom of the room. The other big seller was soft ice cream, and popcorn was a poor third. The place filled up for the first show with almost everybody in town, it seemed, and when we left it looked like the rest of the populace had lined up outside for the second show. Many little boys took over the first four rows of seats, our two youngest among them. We noticed that they had made some fast friends, judging by the shoving, poking, and arm twining going on.

At 9:30 we left the movie, still laughing, and stepped into broad daylight. As we waited for Brian and Linc to join us we could hear them saying "So long—see ya" to their new pals, but later Linc turned to his dad and said with a look of ineffable sadness, "Gee, I guess I won't ever see my friends again."

His dad smiled down at him, but it was Brian who said, "Don't worry, Linc. Maybe we'll make some more friends down the river."

That boy must have used a crystal ball.

3 «
MOSQUITOES

From midnight to 5:00 a.m. we rode the bus, through a night that was never really night at all, for the sun barely dipped below the horizon. We stopped at the Royal Canadian Mounted Police station in Fort Providence, the start of the chain of villages strung the length of the Mackenzie, which still bore testimony in the name "Fort" to the wild days of the 18th and 19th centuries. These were the settlements founded by the "North West Fur Company of Montreal" in competition with "The Governor and Company of Adventurers of England Trading into Hudson's Bay," before they resolved their differences and merged in 1821.

Here we unloaded our many parcels, and started to carry things down the bank to the Mounties' floating dock. Mosquitoes swarmed around us. For the first of many occasions we put on head nets and repellent so that we could work in relative peace. And work we did, for three solid hours. Each boat was loaded and launched when Nick noticed water in the bottom of mine. A leak so soon? Nothing to do but haul the boat out, unload everything, turn it over, and get out the repair kit.

Repairing the bottom of a rubberized canvas kayak is just like putting a patch on a bicycle inner tube. In an emergency you can even stick a Band-aid over a small hole and it will do for awhile. But we were so tired and so annoyed that this minor inconvenience was looking like a major catastrophe. Then Nick suggested we forget the leak until after breakfast. What a thought! I hadn't realized how hungry I was, and all the rest of the family were starving too. There was a little place by the name of "Snowshoe Inn" just down the road from the Mountie station. We left our belongings and walked to the store. Oh consternation! Oh hunger pangs! Oh hours of starving on the steps slapping mosquitoes! On the door was a sign which read "Open 10:00 a.m."

At this point Mr. Sieg Philipps, the owner, came from behind the building and greeted us. "We're not open 'til 10:00 but if you want to you can cook your own!"

Where in our area back home, we wondered, would a restaurant proprietor extend such an invitation to total strangers! Fort Providence is a very small settlement by our standards, and in keeping with this size the Snowshoe Inn is very small too, the only restaurant in town. We were later to be in towns that had no public dining places of any kind, a novel experience indeed for people used to picking and choosing from nearly limitless sources. Even so, we felt Sieg's gesture of hospitality to be one of unusual graciousness.

The Inn had a counter with seven stools. The kitchen was to the right, and a magazine counter and juke box to the left. There was electricity and running water. To the sound of Hawaiian music and Beatle records Nick and I soon had put together a breakfast of fruit, bacon and eggs, toast, and coffee. Sieg stopped his work (carpentry — he was remodeling) long enough to eat the portions we had cooked for him. After the second cup of coffee, Mrs. Philipps (Memoree) came in to thank us for feeding her husband and to apologize for making us do all the work. We thanked them back for allowing us the privilege. By this time we were on such cordial terms that we were like old acquaintances, but this was just the first of many such encounters with people in this amazing country.

Sieg and Memoree are "free traders." That is to say, they are independent store owners and traders, not employed by Hudson's Bay or subsidized by the government. They had been in Fort Providence about three years, and had decided to take the steps that would probably result in a lifetime commitment to this land. They bought the property on which their store stood, an adjoining warehouse which they are enlarging, a craft shop next door, and a home. They have three very small children. With their youth and ambition they are truly modern pioneers. Many times we were to meet and see young families of their age. Most of these are people employed by the government, contracting for a year or two at a time, and often just counting the days until they can go Outside again to live. Private enterprise in the Far North is a relatively rare phenomenon, except for independent oil exploration and development companies which have at least a good fanny-pat from the government. Most of the dollar economy of the Northwest Territories owes its initiative and being to government subsidy, but Sieg and Memoree represent the kind of enterprise that this same government would like to see throughout the whole Territory.

Nick and the boys went back to repair the boat while Memoree and I continued visiting. We looked at the craft shop in which she retailed native handiwork and provided instruction in skills that had almost died out among the Indians. Particularly interesting was the work in porcupine quills, beads, and embroidery. Outside the store was a public address system and a platform for dancing. Memoree said that the young people of the community had helped make the setup and that they had practically a teen center there during the vacation months.

Soon it was time for me to join the family. We walked to the R. C. M. P. station and gave the men a résumé of our itinerary, and an estimated time of arrival at Fort Simpson, almost 165 miles away.

Devon expressed his emotions in a letter home:

"The time is getting very close to leave. I feel a slight (maybe not so slight) uneasiness — not necessarily about the danger since, God knows, there are more dangerous undertakings in this world — but about the step off into the unknown. I think we are up to any situation, but the element of the unknown adds a foreboding, and an exhilaration."

I know I felt much the same way, but my log only records: "Checked out with the Mounties, then off to the beginning of Mills Lake 17 miles downstream."

Brian's diary reads, "We went 17 miles today by kayaks," but Linc goes into more detail: "We had a few difficulties in starting out. A hole developed but we filled it out with some rubber cement."

After three years of plans and dreams we were on the river, on a beautiful balmy summer morning: temperature in the 70's, air fine and still, typical cloud-bedecked blue Canadian sky. Devon had a single kayak, named the *Vanguard* and paddled alone. Nick was in *Flagship* and I was in *Convoy*. Ours were double kayaks, and each of us carried a boy as a bow paddler. Brian and Linc lead lives of interminable bickering interspersed with pleasant sweet oases of deep fraternal friendship. Nick and I learned a long time ago the pairing off which produced the least friction. Brian, who so strongly resembles his father, always rides in my kayak. Lincoln, whose personality is so much like mine, rides with Nick.

What a glorious feeling! The weeks stretched endlessly ahead of us—ten of them. The miles, almost eleven hundred, were endless too. What adventures awaited us? What worlds to conquer? What victories and defeats to add zest to the living?

Our first break from paddling came at lunch when we pulled over to a gravel bank and feasted on cheese and crackers, dried fruit, peanuts, punch, and candy bars. Using my life jacket for a pillow I stretched out and relaxed. Nick and Dev wet a line for a while. Brian and Linc threw rocks, to see how many skippers they could make and to scare the fish into biting, I guess. In an hour we were on our way again, still glorying and exulting in this, our first day.

By 4:30 or 5:00 we were ready for a camp, and here we made our first mistake, one not to be willingly repeated ever again: we camped in the brush. The site looked good: a deserted Indian fish camp, with plenty of wood for fire, a beach for the boats, and a cleared spot among the willows. But by the time we had our camp well under way, we were regretting our selection. Mosquitoes in numbers I've never dreamed possible swarmed into us, and near chaos resulted.

You read about mosquitoes like this, intellectually you appreciate the phenomenon. Experience with quite a few mosquitoes gives you a hint. Actually you feel competent to deal with the pests on the basis of this intellectualization and experience, but until you have run into the millions and billions and trillions of these pests all at once in one spot as we did, you just don't *believe!* These demons must have worn hypodermics made of steel tubing at least. They didn't hover around looking for a juicy spot on your bare skin but came boring in with their suction already working. Hats, pants, shirts, hair, skin—it didn't matter where or what. They tried to bore through to the blood and numbers of them succeeded. On our lower extremities we were wearing new jeans, tennis shoes, and heavy sox. The shoes stopped the creatures, but they got through the sox easily and the jeans without much additional work. The long-sleeved cotton T-shirts we wore were as effective as the sox, namely, not at all. The headnets were fine where the net part hung down, but if any of the hat part contacted the head the mosquitoes bored through cotton, hair, and all. We couldn't get to our gloves and heavier clothing until the tents were up. Mosquito repellent discouraged 99% of the mosquitoes, but when you're numbering quadrillions that leaves thousands able to bite.

I hurried the cook fire, knowing that smoke repels and discourages all insects. Numerous discouraged and doomed ones managed to break through the smoke and die happy, full of my blood, but killed by the smoke: truly a Pyrrhic victory. It promised to be a rugged evening.

As soon as the big tent was erected all five of us scrambled inside hauling our knapsacks with us. We slapped and swatted and smeared the dozens of heedless insects that entered with us. Then we unsympathetically compared bites, each seeking to outdo the other in agonies endured. The cook fire guttered out. The mosquitoes took up battle stations on the tent screen, plastering it almost solid.

Linc sat on the floor of the tent and raged. "They're monsters. They're horrible bloodthirsty monsters." He shuddered in fear.

Brian regarded him sympathetically. "Here. Try this. It will make the bites feel better." He handed him the spray-on Unguentine.

"Shall we pack up and move?" Nick asked.

"I'm too tired," Dev answered, "and I don't suppose we'd have much chance of finding a better spot on Mills Lake."

Nick looked at me. "What do you say, Dear?"

"Let's cope," I voted. "Who are we to let a rotten bunch of mosquitoes tell us what to do?"

So we coped.

Out came the first-aid kit. Nupercainal and Desitin helped take the itch from particularly bothersome bites. Nick and Devon and I put on our "armor"—double-lined bush pants, boots, double-thickness hooded sweatshirts, with the hoods up, gloves, headnet, and repellent. No mosquito could reach skin now. We emerged, the men to finish camp chores and I to cook the dinner. The little boys decontaminated the big tent and settled down with comic books. Unfortunately for me the temperature was now in the low 80's so I was being cooked right along with the dinner, but fairly soon we were seated on the floor of the tent gobbling down our first Mackenzie dinner: freeze-dry steak, German-fried potatoes, fruit cocktail, biscuits, butter, jam, chocolate, and coffee. It was wonderful. We were safe from the winged monsters and our appetites were appeased.

Time for sleep, and all of us were ready, except for one difficult problem: how to perform our evening bathroom duties when menaced as we were? The answer: put your trust in 6-12, Off, Mosquitone, Guard, or whatever your favorite brand of repellent. Slather it on where common sense indicates, and have confidence. It works. It really does!

And so to bed, to sleep, lulled by amazing unusual sounds. Have you ever slept inside a beehive? Who has? But I judge that the sound of those mosquitoes, forming a huge cone-shaped cloud over our tent with its apex extending I know not how high into space, must have been like the center of a hive.

I finally slept, but I remember thinking before sleep finally came, "Thank heavens for good equipment, past experience, and these wonderful, adaptable people. After tonight mosquitoes can never again get us down. We've beaten them—we've coped."

As it turned out, this was true.

Yellowknife, capital of the Northwest Territories, looking up the main street. This picture was taken one hour before midnight on June 22nd. The Canadian flag on the hotel flies day and night.

At Fort Providence the size of the river startled us. The distance to the far shore, an island, is one mile; another mile of water lies on the other side. To the right stretches 1000 miles of river and the nearest town with modern communication Outside is the tiny Indian village of Jean Marie Creek, 115 miles distant.

Wood gatherer (Lincoln) and cook hover over the preparation of the evening meal. The black box in the center is a folding oven. The clear breezy beach guarantees few mosquitoes. Shiny boots and clean pants testify that this picture was taken early in the trip.

Lincoln and Devon hurry into rainwear in the face of an approaching squall. This one's ferocity we under-estimated, and it taught us a never-to-be-forgotten lesson.

Devon bunked alone in a one-man "pop" tent. He carried this tent, his sleeping bag, duffel bag, book bag, and a full sized guitar in his small one-man kayak, and still had room to stretch his legs.

In full bush armor the family prepares to leave the relatively mosquito-free shore for a trek into the bush. Devon carries the rifle in case of bears.

Mills Lake seems to stretch away forever as we make our laborious crossing. Devon, in foreground, rests a bit to look in admiration at the sky.

4 «
MILLS LAKE

On the morning of the second day we faced our first real
hazard of the trip: the crossing of Mills Lake. This lake is really
just a wide spot in the bend of the river, but what a width and
what a bend! Depending on how we measured it we found the
lake to be anywhere from 15 to 30 miles long. The land here
was extremely flat and the river widened and widened until,
as it turned westward, we finally recognized that we were truly
on more of a lake than a river. The water stretched away on
either side to a width of seven or eight miles and far beyond
the horizon in front of us. We never could judge exactly when
to say Mills Lake had "begun" and "ended" but it made little
difference. We had to paddle it all.

Back in Edmonton Nick had sought out the weather room
at the Industrial Airport and questioned the meteorologist about
the forecast for the week. Together they looked at the maps
and talked about isobars and fronts and atmospheric disturb-
ances while I tried to look comprehending. At last we learned
that the forecast was good, no storms were predicted for the
next week. As we moved out across the center of the lake we
felt lucky: the weather was perfect.

The water looked like a vast mirror, as in Coleridge's *Ancient Mariner*, "nor breath, nor motion. . . ." and we felt like
"painted ships upon a painted ocean." The air temperature rose
to the 80's. We had planned to buy headgear in Yellowknife,
but couldn't because of "early closing day," so we used our
mosquito headnets for shade. These together with dark glasses
were quite effective if not exactly handsome protection from
the brightness. The steady rhythm of our paddles made me
sing along inside, but every now and then I forgot to conserve
my energy and burst out loud with song, a round we used to

25

sing at canoe camp: "Our paddles clean and bright, flashing like silver . . ."

As we neared the mid-point of the lake we kept looking for the channel marker buoys that we knew were around somewhere. The flatness of lake and surrounding landscape produced odd optical illusions. We saw mirages, usually in the form of shimmering walls of water in the distance. The first time we saw a pair of black ducks on the water we thought they were marker buoys. And when we finally did see a marker buoy it looked like a smokestack of a tugboat. Only when the "smokestack" had shrunk to a ridiculous size and the "boat" had persistently failed to appear did we realize we'd spotted our first marker and were on course.

The cloud formations defied description. Almost never is a far northern Canadian sky totally free of clouds in summer. They drift and build, group and regroup, scud and pause, spread out and tower. We worried not at all about the great mounds of whipped cream clouds until the tell-tale anvil formation sprouted. Then we watched for a change in color at the bottom, from white to dull grey to black, and for the curtain of rain which hung like a shadow below clouds like these. On this day all these ominous formations were walking far to the northeast, and little by little we grew confident that we would make the crossing safely.

From meeting an occasional pair of ducks we now started to move among flocks, first of dozens, then of hundreds. Most of these were now barely flying either because of the molting season or because they had just learned how to fly, and they moved, staying close to the water, only far enough to feel safe from our approach. A look at our bird book identified them as coots, teal and canvas backs. I am convinced we saw wood ducks too, but the rest of the family views this conviction with skepticism. Each boat carried a pair of field glasses and we were constantly pausing to stare and emote at this amazing quantity of bird life.

The time dragged on and we kept those paddles chunking, thankful for the weather but missing the balm of a cooling breeze. However, we dared not complain aloud lest we tempt fate. A government pamphlet describing Mills Lake says "Care must be taken in crossing Mills Lake as sudden storms create bad canoeing conditions in the shallow water. If conditions are dangerous the canoeist should pull to shore and wait for better weather." We were miles from any shore and at this time had no way of knowing whether "sudden storms" meant ones that pounced with ten minutes' warning or an hour and ten minutes. Without current our paddling speed is about two miles per hour, but we can probably sprint for a while at three or four. In the center of Mills Lake there is just no place to hide.

By late afternoon we had covered 12 miles. The shorelines were noticeably drawing in and we knew it was time to look for a camp. We made the long pull to the nearest shore at our left almost two miles distant and found a likely spot on a sand bar. A thick covering of leaves made a soft floor and promised more comfortable sleeping than plain ground. The mosquitoes attacked in force the moment we landed, but this time we were ready. Devon even found out he could crawl into his collapsed one-man tent and assemble it from inside. Inasmuch as the shelter when up is about 36 inches high, and has the ground dimensions of a sleeping bag, this was quite a feat. It was also a pretty hysterical performance to watch, which we did with great shouts of encouragement. Finally, though, Dev's tent was up, screen zipped tight shut, and Dev seated triumphantly inside while we still stood outside among the insects, so we stopped laughing and put up the big tent.

Devon at nineteen was a joy to have along on this vacation, probably his last with the family. He seems on casual acquaintance to be very much a scholar, with his horn-rimmed glasses and his soft-spoken manner; but he is a rugged five foot eleven with the muscles of a logger. His major in college is forestry. He excels in skiing, fencing, cycling, and outdoor living. He is also an accomplished guitarist with a fine singing voice. Very much his own master, and of course missing the girl back home, Devon was often a loner in the midst of family. But he never shirked the many chores there were to do, and his shrewd judgment was of unmeasured help to Nick in making decisions and in at least one instance was a real life saver.

After dinner we chattered away at a great pace over the day's marvels. One of them was the size of the stone flies in this part of the country—monsters two to three inches long! In the morning we found over a dozen of them dead on the tent screen, and Devon, the naturalist of the family, said that the mosquitoes had killed them in lieu of us. He said they don't have to have red blood to exist, insect fluids will do. I learned later that he was putting us on.

Our second day on the lake was as calm, beautiful and exhausting as the first. We followed more closely along the shore and again were astonished by the water fowl. Particularly thrilling was the sound of coots taking off, a whistling, popping birdcall, but our bird book tells us this peculiar sound is made by their wings. All over the lake as we paddled along we could hear this sound as flock after flock took to the air.

The day wore on. Arms, legs, backs—all grew tired. A look at the map showed us we were within three miles of a place earlier marked as a possible camp: "Mills Lake Airport—abandoned." Should we try for it? A family conference, in which I declined to vote, favored the effort, so on we worked. I thought the hour and a half would never end. A spot between my shoulder blades ached so badly it finally felt numb, and then I couldn't feel it at all. This was more alarming than aching. About the time I was wondering if perhaps my shoulder blades had dropped off, the abandoned airport came into sight, and we knew we had a winner.

We beached on a sandy shingle on a little gravel point just as a small breeze started, so scarcely a mosquito found us. The brush did not begin for several hundred yards where a steep bank led up to the airport. A little farther along a derelict tug stood among the tangle of wild roses, the first invitation to go exploring. Quickly we put up the big tent while Devon set up his small one and, forgetting our tired state, we scrambled up the bank to the abandoned boat, in our excitement leaving behind our headnets and cameras.

For the next hour we wandered, exclaimed, slapped mosquitoes (there were plenty of them among the weeds), and theorized over what seemed to be an old World War II air installation. Dilapidated Quonset huts, still carrying army air corps designations, lined what was obviously a workshop area. One building even bore the stenciled word CANOL, a sure sign of the war. It was easy to find the runway, now heavily over-grown, but with a G.I.-devised contraption of steel drums for smoothing the lumpy surface, trailer hitch intact, still standing in readiness at the end. We found garages and barracks, refuse pits, a couple of broken-down trucks (all stripped of useful parts), two more small tugs, without engines, of course, and too many mosquitoes. The latter and our returning tiredness and our appetites finally drove us back to camp.

A little breeze came up after dinner, sweeping the beach clean of mosquitoes and for the first time we could stay outside the tent minus heavy sweatshirts and bothersome headnets. Dev broke out the spinning gear and started casting as an im-mense flock of geese flew over. Brian and Linc built a freeway in the sand. Nick and I stood close together sipping hot mugs of boiled camp coffee, the absolute rulers of all we surveyed. At this moment Dev, with the wildest of whoops, pulled in the first fish of the summer: a huge northern pike.

My log book carries this comment for the day: "Boy, are we having fun, and am I bushed!" For me the real part of the vacation had truly begun.

In the morning we were able to eat our first cooked meal outside the tent. We slow-poked our way through camp chores and got under way by 11:30. This was to be, in the future, a regular occurrence for us. Even when we promised ourselves an early start we almost always could get on the water no earlier than 11:00 a.m. Finally, we came to refer to this time as the Witching Hour and to relax and enjoy our slothfulness.

On this, our fourth day, we had only about an hour and a half of paddling when the weather changed to blustery and threatening. We made for shore, built a fire, ate lunch, dis-cussed the situation, and fished. Devon caught another beauti-ful pike. The wind kept on, the waves wore white caps, but both wind and waves were at our backs. So we launched the kayaks during a little lull and made some excellent time, keep-ing about fifty feet off shore. A nice thing about a rubberized canvas hull: you can chance many scrapes on rocks and shore bottoms. You may eventually get a leak from a cut or an abrasion, but you won't bash in your boat's hull. And you can't sink these kayaks very easily. They have flotation chambers along their gunwales, and will support a full load even when swamped. These are mighty reassuring features to think about when rollicking along over two-foot combers in a craft that has maybe four inches of freeboard.

That night we had another beautiful campsite, but we were all so worn out that we were in our sleeping bags by 8:15 and asleep by 8:16. It seems that 24 hours of daylight tricks you for a while into expending great amounts of energy and sleeping very little. Then in a week or less the dire need for sleep comes in a swoop. After catching up you then find yourself staying up and active for 18 to 20 hours daily until "swoop," another catching up. I guess that if you live up here all year 'round winter is the time for sleeping.

On our next day we paddled in stormy and threatening weather. With great prescience we pulled to shore for lunch mere seconds before a rain squall hit us. Quickly we had a huge fire going, one that would dry up rain and drive off mosquitoes with equal efficiency.

Camp that night was on a pretty little shingled beach. As we drifted off to sleep Nick remarked, "The first night I couldn't get comfortable no matter how I moved around. Now I can't get UN-comfortable!"

Snuggling down onto my one-half inch thickness of foam mattress I murmured agreement.

Interesting always on these far-away trips are the sounds alien to nature such as those made by a distant plane, boat, helicopter, chain saw, compressor, gun, and so on. Soon we learned to identify plane and helicopter, and differentiate outboard motors, or "kickers" as they are universally called here. On the morning of our sixth day, just as we were launching, we heard another curious motor sound. This one had a deep rhythmic throbbing to it unlike any we had ever heard before. Soon the boat was in sight and in just a few minutes we were overtaken by our first Mackenzie River tugboat: the bulky, powerful, wonderful Diesel *Tembah*, an Indian name meaning "Rapids". Captained by Mr. Nelson, this boat is responsible for all the channel marking on the Mackenzie from Norman

Wells to Yellowknife. It has a special bow, capable of lifting and placing heavy buoys in the river, and its powerful engines are more than a match for any current the river offers. A huge, sweeping, glassed-in pilothouse and modern radar make navigation possible under extremely trying conditions. But even the *Tembah*, Captain Nelson told us, pulls to shore and rides out the mean squalls and storms that hit the river when the north wind blows in earnest.

The *Tembah* came alongside us during the morning's lull. She cut her engines and idled quietly, just enough to keep her way in the current. A half-dozen of her crew stared down at us from her rails while we stared back from our water-level seats. Then ensued one of those typically-cordial Mackenzie hospitality conversations, and by its end ten minutes later, we knew we'd found some new friends.

After introductions and time-of-day chatter Captain Nelson offered to carry a message to Fort Simpson to the R.C.M.P. to report we were well and safe. He also told us he would keep watch for us, and if ever we needed help of any kind while the *Tembah* was passing by to signal with a dish towel and he'd be there. He warned us sternly to keep being wary of river squalls—that to underestimate their treachery was many a boatman's undoing. And finally he promised to look for us at Fort Simpson should we be there at the same time as the *Tembah*.

With a toot of the whistle, *Tembah* pulled away. As if on signal the staring crew came to life and sprang away from the rails to disappear to their duty stations, or so we thought. Seconds later they were all back again, each man with a camera in hand, leaning over the stern railings taking pictures of us. About this time we remembered our cameras and scrambled them into action. So all of us have pictures of people taking pictures, most of them out of focus and too distant.

It was a long paddle this day, often against contrary winds. The last mile seemed as long as the first ten to me. But when we landed at what was once Browning's Sawmill and Farm, I knew the aching muscles were worth it.

5 «

BROWNING'S FARM

I used to think that a good place to camp would be in a deserted cabin. This was a long time ago, before I had ever seen one. I have found out that even camping near one is usually a mistake. Deserted cabins leak. They smell of mildew, decay, rotten wood, bird droppings, and worse. Their floors, if they have any, are often ready to collapse into the root cellar. Generally inhospitable, sometimes dangerous, they stimulate my imagination, cry to be explored, but then beg to be left in peace.

Often the land surrounding a deserted cabin gives the same reverse welcome. An old caved-in drainage ditch or garbage dump or privy, overgrown with weeds and wild flowers, becomes a trap like a deadfall. Firewood is often hard to find. Finally, there is rarely a clean, attractive place to pitch a tent or make a cooking fire because the brush comes back quickly to a spot which has been lumbered off and cleared.

We thought we might have to make this kind of camp at Browning's sawmill, but when we got close enough to see the abandoned landing our worries vanished. A wide clean beach of yellow sand sloped gently to the river. Downstream a broken wharf, with a great stack of grey, weathered lumber spilling over its side, formed a large barrier to the current causing a perfect backwater for landing. More and more as we gain experience in river touring we have learned the value of backwaters and how to use them. We have also learned to know when they hamper us, and how then to avoid them. This combination of shingle beach, strong current, and backwater was a campsite-seeking kayaker's delight!

A huge bank of hard-packed, orange hued sawdust about eight feet high overlooked the beach. It spread for fifty yards

Rapidly the diesel tug *Tembah* chugs away after a rendezvous with our three kayaks in mid-stream. The *Tembah* was responsible for channel signs and marker buoys along 500 miles of the Mackenzie.

At Browning's Farm, recently abandoned near Head-of-the-Line, nature gradually wins back the land. Farm implements were stored inside this barn, with harnesses for work horses hanging on the walls.

The author cooks a pancake breakfast in front of the ever-present drying rack. Plentiful driftwood made campfire cookery easy.

out from a tipsy shed, the former sawmill itself. Above and beyond this sawdust another steep bank loomed, covered with green grass, pink roses and other wild flowers. At its top we could see a storehouse to the south and the roof of a large building about two hundred yards to the north.

Nick and Linc, in the leading boat, scared up a bobcat as they landed. They couldn't wait to see if maybe there weren't many more around, so we went exploring at once. Our quick survey of the farm area high on the bluff stirred up nothing except every mosquito in the world, so we fled to the breeze-swept beach, unloaded the boats, and set up camp.

That night, as the rest of the family slept, I lay there in my sleeping bag and watched the weather making. I could see the changing colors on the river, mostly green and greys with touches of blue. Great clouds piled up so that the sky darkened almost to a real night. The wind picked up, and the tent swayed gently, suspended by rubber shock cords in its outer frame. The thrill of the building storm bore in on me and I smiled as I remembered how differently we lived at home.

Wordsworth wrote, "The world is too much with us, late and soon. Getting and spending we lay waste our powers." Here on the mighty Mackenzie the world we regularly lived in was far away. No radio. No television. No telephone. No smog. No traffic. No running water. No gas. No electricity. No refrigeration. No ironing. No menu planning. No shopping. No door-to-door salesmen. No school bells. No commercials. I fell asleep counting "noes".

In the morning we awakened to a sullen sky and a surly wind, but, confident of our ability to assess the weather, we broke camp anyway, all but the big tent, and packed the boats. Some small remnant of self-doubt made us leave up the big tent and move it from its perch high on the sawdust pile to a more sheltered spot on the beach. Just as we were walking off to explore the farm, while Nick was explaining to Linc that the aerodynamic lines of the tent were sufficient insurance against its being blown away, a tremendous gust of wind picked up the tent and hurled it toward the water. Linc earned the hero-title of the day for he was listening to Nick with one doubting ear and watching the tent with one worried eye. With marvelous reflexes and a whoop of dismay he dashed to the water's edge and grabbed a corner of the tent just as it hit the river.

After hauling the tent in and relocating it, we found rocks to hold the corners down. Meanwhile the wind had suddenly ceased and the deadly quiet made us take a more appraising look at the sky. The cloud cover had changed from grey to black, the far shore of the river could not be seen, but from this direction a dark curtain of rain advanced up the river. Again some residual instinct made us feel very uneasy, and without much discussion we decided to get inside the tent and wait and see what was going to happen.

The stillness grew more ominous. Not a ripple stirred the river's surface, but across the way we could see the water curtain move. Then it happened: a quick, sudden riffling of the surface. In seconds the riffles were wavelets, then waves, then huge whitecaps. The dead stillness vanished into howling wind. The wind grew until it literally blew the tops off of the white-caps and flattened the water into the wildest chop I had ever seen. At the same time the cloud deck lowered until at the peak of the gale the sky and water met and visibility was zero.

One, two, perhaps three minutes passed. The clouds began to lift; a tiny change in the sound of the wind, a little falling off in its force, continuing, progressing, gradually quieting, until, indeed, the squall passed over. All of us knew at last the meaning of the phrase "the lull before the storm." And now we also knew what the government pamphlet had tried to tell us about "bad canoeing conditions" and why Captain Nelson of the *Tembah* had cautioned us so earnestly. We talked for a while about what we had just seen.

What should you do if you were ever stupid enough to get caught in a kayak in a squall? There seemed to be only one answer: "Turn into the wind and ride it out." But as we left the shelter to go exploring and photographing the farm, we all told ourselves how we should hate to get caught in a storm like that, and promised ourselves we never would. Firm in our good intentions, and confident we would never lay another yard of concrete on that well-paved road, we scrambled up the bank to see what was left of the farm of "F. J. Browning,

Grower of Vegetables, Head-of-the-Line, Mackenzie River,
N.W.T."

On our way to the top we came across a large shaft or cave
excavated far into the bank and reinforced with heavy timbers.
A little deduction and we concluded it had been a storage
cave, probably for grain and vegetables. Above the cave we
found a small building made of logs which had been a trading
post and store. The counter and shelves were still in place with
a litter of small, useless objects all about. There were damp
packets of seeds, a few old bills, and several tiny bottles of
tonic called "Dutch Drops," whose label stated these were a
marvelous patent medicine claiming to cure practically everything from angina to warts, but we resisted the temptation to
stock up and continued our exploring.

Next to the store was another small storehouse, this one
with several sacks of grain and large beans. Then came the
big building whose roof we had seen from the river. A tall pole,
once carrying an aerial, stretched up from the front gable. This,
then, was the main farmhouse. We reached it just in time to
shelter from a shower and found out that even though the
home had not been lived in for several years the roof was still
fairly tight. We found a large stove in the kitchen still capable
of being stoked, but the shower had passed over so we resumed
our walk.

To the rear of the farmhouse were three fairly large buildings. Two proved to be homes, and the third a repair shop. The
homes were practically empty, but in the repair shop we found
a great quantity of tools and equipment. It looked as if even
now a person could fix a harness, a dog-sled runner, a chain
saw, or even a kicker with the spare parts available.

Now we turned toward the barn and stable buildings several hundred yards across a partly-fenced field. They made a
beautiful sight in the summer rain with their pale grey weathered log sides and sod roofs. Inside the barns we found harnesses in perfect condition, farm implements aplenty. Obviously
there had been horses and cows stabled here. We even found
what must have been the dairy as evidenced by the remains
of a cream separator. Then we came back to the farmhouse
again to wait out the next shower.

While the little boys exclaimed over a cache of children's toys they discovered in the attic, and Nick and Dev discussed the farming operation itself, I stood in the front doorway and tried to imagine what it could have been like living here twenty years ago. In my mind's eye I watched my children running across the field to the corrals by the barn where my man was climbing down from the cultivator, about to unhitch one of our huge farm horses. He waved to me, and I waved back, seeing the children now safe in their father's care, and turned toward the kitchen where good smells of freshly-baking bread were coming from the oven of my sturdy wood stove. . . .

There had been a Browning family raised here. Many years ago F. J. Browning emigrated from the States and carved out this farm. A dedicated farmer, he knew the land was fruitful in spite of permafrost and the short growing season. By use of muscle and brain power he learned to grow many things, first on a scale to support his family and then commercially. He added a sawmill to his business enterprises, cut his own timber, and dressed his own lumber. Vegetables, grain, dairy products, lumber, all required labor and he hired labor among the native Indians. He chose an Indian woman for his wife, and their children grew to become respected all up and down the river. He had great love for the Mackenzie and great faith in the ability of its people to live in this stern land. He knew they could adapt their lives to the tremendous changes brought by the white man, that a prosperous abundant living is here in the Mackenzie region for anyone willing to work for it. He never underestimated the amount of work necessary, however, and deplored the tendency of people to lean more and more on the government dole.

Tragedy overtook Browning in the spring of 1966. Having abandoned this farm at Head-of-the-Line he was killed in a bulldozer upset while working at his new farm and mill farther down the river. I pondered these things while gazing across the unplowed fields of the old farm when one of our sons came up to me with a Christmas card he had found among the scattered papers in the attic. As I read the card I knew the summary was there. It was a quotation from Whittier:

"Man trespassed here; but Nature lost
No sight of her domain.
She waited and she brought the old
Wild beauty back again."

The date on the card was Christmas, 1939.

The shower ended, so we left the farmhouse and walked toward the bank. At its edge we looked up and down and across the river and, suddenly realizing the air and water were much too calm, we ran pell-mell for the tent. We reached it just in time. Again we were amazed at the fury of the squall. I shuddered at the thought of a tiny cockleshell boat being driven by the wind. No matter. We were safe and dry and far from being out in any storm. "That's my idea of nothing to do," I murmured to no one in particular.

"Yeah, what you said—some of that," Devon muttered back as we just stared at the vanishing river. Nick had one arm around each of the younger boys who filled the air with gee-whizzes and gollies.

And then, almost all of a sudden, it passed.

"Let's saddle up," Nick hollered as we clambered out into a brightening sky.

In five minutes we were on the river, now calmed, paddling along the shore of the Mackenzie toward the mouth of the Trout River where it entered a mile or so below Browning's. We knew that by staying near the shore we could reach the banks if menaced by a sudden squall, so we enjoyed the exciting cloudwork in the sky and set an easy but steady pace with our paddles.

I don't know what was wrong with me, but when we reached the Trout River entrance I was feeling grouchy. Nick was ahead a few lengths and Devon beside him. I looked up at the weather and called out, "We'd better stop here," but when Nick called back, "Let's try for the next point," I felt too grumpy to argue. I knew we couldn't make it. I just knew.

But we started across the quarter mile with the great expanse of the Mackenzie on our right and the Trout pouring in on our left. No shore to reach but the one opposite, once we were committed.

Devon, in his lighter single kayak, made excellent time and was never in doubt or danger. Nick and Linc, the bigger, stronger combination, putted right along and drew steadily ahead of Brian and me. Brian and I gave it our best and kept moving well, but at the point of no return I got that old feeling we have come to describe as "paddling scared." I looked up at the sky to my right, then leaned into my stroke and called out to Brian, "Come on, Son, let's dig!"

And we did. Our pace picked up from firm and steady to a real sprint, but I knew we were losing.

"Briny," I said, trying to conceal the fear in my voice, "We're not going to make it. What do we do if we get caught in a squall?"

"Turn into the wind and ride it out," he called back.

"Dig," I hollered, "Dig, and pull, and pull, and pull."

Harder and faster we sped along. But now the sky was black, the wind was gone, the water was glass. Not a sound anywhere but that of our own making.

"Pull, Honey, pull," I called. We had a hundred yards to go.

"Devon's made it," Brian shouted. I felt a little breeze.

"Here it comes, son. Let's keep working!" But I knew it wasn't any use. Ahead of us the edge of the squall hit Nick and Linc. They had about twenty feet to go, and in a mad flurry of paddle blades they managed to reach shore. Their boat was almost swamped by waves pouring in, and they were drenched, but their feet were on solid ground.

Meanwhile the edge of the wind hit us. We were only fifty yards from safety but we may as well have been fifty miles.

"Here we go," I yelled, and with one powerful backwater on the right I turned us head on into the wind.

The rest is a haze of fear and exhilaration. We sat there and rode out that storm like the most rugged pair of old pros you'd ever want to shake a paddle at. As the waves surged by on either side the little kayak just undulated gently. With pressure on the paddle blade it was easy to keep her headed into the wind although I felt the wood give and wondered if the paddle might not break.

"How ya doin', Brian?"

"Fine," he hollered back.

The wind mounted to a scream. The clouds came down to the water. The waves were flattened. I couldn't even keep my eyes open against the blast.

"Yubba dubba dooo," I whooped, and Brian "yubbadubbad" right back.

"We're doing okay, we're going to make it fine." I wondered whose courage I was building as I shouted on. But Brian's reply showed not one shred of fear.

Then the first signs of abatement came, and I called, "It's letting up. We're over the worst! Hooray!"

Back in a flash came Brian's jubilant shout: "Let's go back and do it again!"

You've got to like a boy like that!

Little by little the cloud lifted. The wind died down. The shore came into sight. Devon was high on a hillock scanning the river for us. Linc and Nick were running along the edge of the shore. They saw us. We saw them. Great shouting all around. We had been blown upstream into the Trout River almost three hundred yards.

When we came to shore there was much rejoicing all around with play-by-play recounting of what we did and how. They said the worst part was when we passed out of sight. We said the worst part was just before the squall really hit.

Wet and soppy, we soon made a huge, roaring fire, and as we dried out, ate our lunch and grumbled at the weather. We took to the river one more time to cross it during a lull between storms, but we made camp after paddling for less than an hour because the rain bore down again.

That day we made only two miles.

6 «

JEAN MARIE CREEK

"Hey, what's that noise?" I shouted, jumping to my feet.

"It sounds like a jet — far off," said Devon.

We knew that we were nowhere near an area where jet planes flew, but we all stood and stared high and hard to the north, straining with our ears to pinpoint the sound.

"Migosh, look!" Linc exclaimed, waving his arms wildly. Across the water toward the mouth of the Trout River at least a hundred geese flew north at an altitude of around 750 feet. The jet-like whisper of their wings faded from hearing as they in turn faded from sight. We were as thrilled as if we had invented them. So began a great day. Our maps showed we were less than thirty miles from Jean Marie Creek. Although it had taken us seven days to travel eighty-nine miles, we had now entered a sixty-mile section of the river where the current picked up to six and seven miles per hour. With the weather so clear we knew we could reach the Indian village by supper time.

It was a glorious paddle. About 4:30 p.m. we came around a curve and sighted the village. Probably in the same instant one of the villagers sighted us. A half an hour later we pulled up on shore under the curious stares of at least two dozen Indian men and children lined up on the bank above the beach. Standing with them was a white man.

We beached the boats and climbed out. The man walked down to greet us.

"Hi," said my husband, "we're the Nickersons."

"I'm Victor Monus. Welcome," was the reply.

Soon introductions were over, Linc and Brian were making friendly noises with a group of Indians about their ages, and

Devon had secured the kayaks. Mr. Monus suggested a cup of coffee, so we followed him up the beach.

At the top of the bank the whole village of Jean Marie could be caught in one sweeping glance. It looked not at all like what I expected, although I can't say exactly what I did expect. (A scattering of tents, I supposed, arranged at random, and maybe out-of-doors fires?) Instead I could see two rows of neat, well-ordered houses, constructed of squared logs, which lined a wide graveled street. A second street came into the first at an angle, and along this street were more tidy homes, and a good-sized white-painted school. Rising above the school was a ninety-foot steel radio tower. The final surprise was the two large street lights suspended from very new-looking poles.

Mr. Monus led us through the yards of a couple of homes on the way to his own. Although a gaggle of sub-teen girls and boys followed at our heels, the women and tiny children were either safely hidden away in their homes or retreating behind slowly closing doors, but there were dark curious eyes watching from the curtained windows. The men and teen-age boys, however, were casually sitting on their front porches, not quite looking in our direction. We smiled and said "hello" and were rewarded by direct looks, returned smiles, and greetings. Later Mr. Monus told us this was just the right thing to do. We needed this approval. We still felt ill at ease in our "strangers in a far country" role, and were only acting on a theory of behavior which says: Be courteous and say the first friendly words. You can't make the situation worse by such behavior, and you just might make it a lot better.

Soon we reached another tiny log house and met Mrs. Monus (Anita) and their two-year-old daughter, Kathy.

"Do come in and have some coffee. You must be cold after being on the river."

It felt strange to be seated indoors. In just eight days we had grown far more used to the outdoors than we realized. The fired-up stove in the little room soon had us shedding our sweaters, but we were still too warm. Later we found that almost all indoors in the Far North were kept too warm to suit us. Was this, indeed, because we were so used to camping out?

Or was it perhaps because even in the summertime the people still haven't quite warmed up from their sixty-below winters and keep their houses overheated?

The conversation was rolling. We were all enjoying ourselves. We told Vic and Anita that we planned to stay the night, and asked permission to camp on the beach. They were delighted. We left to do our many camp jobs but with an invitation to come back for coffee and cake.

Down to the beach we walked with Indian children streaming along behind us. We tackled our unloading and settling jobs eagerly. Strange how my mood had changed from an hour before! When we landed at Jean Marie I didn't want to stay at all. It took a great effort at self-control to keep from saying "Let's not camp here. Let's go on." Civilization, even as represented here by fifty Indians, a handful of log cabins, and one white family, was almost oppressive. The beach seemed barren, used-up, uninviting. I didn't like to look at a motor-driven scow anchored in my front yard. A couple of empty red plastic oil cans left at the water's edge bothered me too. A stack of squared logs, a cache of gasoline drums, a tangled wire cable completed the scene in one direction, and all those curious staring people lived in the other direction.

Now, however, the beach looked fine. Obviously it would be unwise to cook over an open fire with so many inflammables around so I quickly dug out the one-burner "Optimus" stove we had tucked away for just this kind of occasion. By the time camp was buttoned down, dinner was served. Naturally enough the "curious staring people" had gone home long ago to their own dinners. I wondered if maybe I hadn't done at least fifty per cent of the staring and shown a good one-half of the curiosity myself.

Dishes done, we walked up the slope to the Monus house, picking up four little Indians on the way as trailers. Vic and Anita invited us all in, the children sat on the floor, the rest of us on chairs and benches, while Anita went back to hovering over her oven. She cooked on a Coleman stove, and was baking with a tricky, cranky oven which sat on top of the burners. For three years she had been on fighting terms with that oven, and wasn't about to let it win this skirmish. Soon she appeared with three pans, each with a different kind of cake. We feasted.

Meanwhile a little Indian girl noticed my camp purse, a homely plastic thing on a shoulder strap. I could see her eying it, so I started rummaging through it. First I pulled out my reading glasses and put them on. Then I took out a pencil. Then a notebook. Next a large comb, and a metal mirror in a plastic case. Bobbie pins. Sewing kit. Hand cream. Cub Scout knife. Lipstick. Chapstick. Wallet. Checkbook. A dozen more trivial items. These were all passed around from hand to hand and properly exclaimed over. Finally — a handful of bubble gum!

Bubble gum, cake, coffee, and conversation: the evening flew by. We learned that Victor and Anita Monus were Wycliffe Bible Translators, originally from the United States, who had spent the past three years at Jean Marie studying the dialect of the particular band of Slavey Indians in this area. Just exactly what other missionary duties they perform was never made clear, but Victor spoke of several self-help projects in the village. First the sawmill, owned in common, was bringing a lot of work to the men and older boys. In addition to squaring timbers for their own village they had contracted to supply cut logs to new Fort Wrigley now under construction miles downstream. Next, a well had been dug near the center of the village and would soon be supplying pure water to all. Perhaps one day it would even be piped to the homes, but at any rate, a town pump was a great improvement over dipping water from the river. Vic showed us the quaint yoke with its two large buckets that he used in carrying the daily water supply at least a quarter of a mile to his home. Finally, we were told about a tugboat that had only just been bought, so new an addition it had not even been put into operation but was still beached waiting for its new owners to be trained in its handling. The street lights had been installed this year, and would provide much comfort in the almost 24 hours of darkness during the winter season. Street lights implied a power source, and this was supplied by a gasoline generator which had recently been installed. A combination firebreak and airstrip was also shown to us. We left the Monuses in the pale light of midnight, pleased with our new friends and impatient for morning.

I slept until seven, having been disturbed only a little by the sound of frenzied barking around 4:30 a.m. Then at 7:30 I left the tent to start breakfast preparation. Just as I reached our supplies, still cached in the boats, a man and two boys burst out of a nearby cabin and ran down the bank, the man carrying a rifle. I could see they were heading for a scow which was beached right next to our kayaks. A quick tug on the motor lanyard and they were off across the river boiling up a furious wake. Nick came out of the tent and asked, "What's doing?"

"I don't know," I said, "why don't you ask one of the other men?"

He walked away to see if he could satisfy his curiosity and mine.

It seems that in public, at least when strange white people are around, Indian women are seldom either seen or heard. I deduced also that if I wanted information from an Indian man it was better, more in keeping, to have one of my men, either Nick or Devon, do the talking for me. It was quite a discipline for this gabby, USA-type female and proved particularly difficult when I felt that the men weren't asking the right questions or pursuing the proper conversational directions. But it was often the only way to find out anything at all, so I was learning to shut up!

Nick came back to tell me that the men of the village had spotted a moose on the opposite shore. Moose meat brings much rejoicing. But this time, no luck: the moose got away.

I turned to my breakfast cooking, and found myself face to face with an unnerving experience. Only years of service as a Cub Scout Den Mother carried me through. No sooner had I starting assembling the breakfast makings than at least ten Indian children materialized from nowhere. They stood around me in a large closed circle and stared and stared. Now and then one would nudge another and say something in Slavey, but they never spoke a word to me, so I went about my work.

The top of my little Optimus burner measures 3 by 3 inches, but my square griddle measured 11½ by 11½ inches, making a neat problem in balance. Things weren't too crucial in the matter of frying bacon, but scrambling the eggs required real concentration. (A griddle, you remember, has no sides like a frying pan.) I wondered if I were up to it. I had planned to bake corn bread in a folding fry pan, but with all those bright faces peering at me and my lack of practice on that wildly-hissing stove I chickened out. Just to add to my uneasiness I saw Anita Monus and her daughter appear at the crest of the bank and start down. Nick and Devon and the boys joined the circle and gawked at the cooking too. So I squatted there on my heels, and stirred up a perfect batch of unscorched scrambled eggs. Such luck! Then Anita came forward and with a shy smile presented a whole loaf of bread saying, "I thought maybe you could use this."

Could we ever! It was a perfect gesture of hospitality I will never forget.

Anita had a "cuppa" with us while we ate breakfast, and soon Victor joined us, wearing his yoke of buckets. The only place we had ever seen such a contraption was in pictures of little Dutch boys. Brian and Lincoln tried it on. They found, to their surprise, that it made water carrying much easier. As water boys on this trip they could appreciate the problem of a daily tote up that hill. Nick, meanwhile, whispered to me that we really should give the Indian children a little treat, so I robbed our next two days' lunches of their hard candy supply, and doled out one piece of cellophane-wrapped candy to each eager little hand. Two of the older girls dashed up the hill and soon returned with their very little sisters. After these girls got their treat they were just as quickly returned to their homes. All of us were having a good time.

When Nick said he wanted to take some "more" pictures the story of the barking dogs unfolded. He had awakened at 4:00 to excellent light and a silent village. What an opportunity for undisturbed camera work! Silently he dressed and hung his cameras and meters about him. Then he quietly pulled down the zipper on the front screen of the tent.

Pandemonium!

Indian settlements, no matter what the size, always have dogs. These animals are staked out on chains in very logical places around a village or a camp. Here at Jean Marie there was was a regular line of them between the beach and the nearest houses. Each home had four or more dogs chained about its yard. The first dog to hear Nick let out the yelp that triggered every other animal in the village, as with the "shot heard 'round the world." A half dozen doors opened and dusky faces peered out. Soon they saw it was only the white stranger wandering around for some reason and the doors were shut again. But within ten minutes Nick felt he had to retreat. He said later that the moment he stepped out of sight, the dogs quieted. "The zipping of the tent screen was just like a switch — they all turned off!"

Now we left our campsite and, together with the Monuses, toured the village. First we walked to the sawmill where a dozen Indian men were working. They looked just like lumbermen in the states, from their safety-toed shoes to their yellow hard hats, except for one thing: warm as the day was, none of them had their sleeves rolled up. I asked Vic about this, thinking perhaps it was protection against insects. He said no, that it was a form of modesty, that the Indian did not go bare-armed. I had my private doubts, but must admit I never saw a bare-armed Indian the length of the Mackenzie, yet I still wonder if Victor's explanation were true.

Next we walked through the whole village to the other end of town and visited the Federal School, a beautiful little structure of white painted logs, bright, clean and airy. Surrounded by the books, desks, blackboards, and smell of chalk I felt as if I had never left home. Brian and Lincoln were busily trying desks to find one their size. Nick and Devon were being introduced to a very intelligent-looking older man who had just entered. I wandered away to see the particular textbooks being used in this graded one to six classroom, and to give the men a chance to talk without a woman present. Believe it or not, I found the books: *Streets and Roads, Our New Friends,* and *Fun with Dick and Jane.* Later Vic said that the federal government was planning to develop textbooks more in keeping with the

Slavey culture, but "Planning" is an expression that names no deadline.

Soon the men came over and introduced Mr. Louis Norwegian, the Chief of the Jean Marie Indian "Band" as it is called, rather than "tribe." His handshake was hearty, and his greeting cordial. "I am Louis Norwegian. I welcome you to Jean Marie." We walked together back through the village.

The younger boys ran on ahead to find their pals. We came up to them all crouched in the dirt making a tight circle, about eight of them. They had a half-grown dog on the ground and were holding it down. One of the Indian boys, Rufus by name, brandished a large hunting knife. The dog they seemed to be sacrificing made no outcry or struggle, and since Mr. Norwegian and the Monuses didn't show any alarm I fought down the urge to interfere and passed by too. I heard a shout of laughter, and soon the circle broke up and the little dog was running free. We learned later that the boys were digging out a tick. The laugh came after the operation when one of the boys suggested, "Now let's cut off an ear!"

Our visit was ending. The weather promised smooth paddling and the current was swift. The date was July 1st, Canada's "Dominion Day" and, although Fort Simpson was 45 miles distant, we thought perhaps we could reach it in time to share in some of the day's last celebrations. Yet we were sorry to leave. There was much more to see and hear in Jean Marie, if only we had had the time. I remembered how, only nine days before, time seemed to stretch endlessly ahead, yet here at our first contact with civilization, we faced the fleetness of time again.

"Goodbye — take care — goodbye." The current caught us and swept us on our way.

7 «
FORT SIMPSON

Long after we left the village the whine of its sawmill followed us, and not until the second hour were we out of earshot. About this time, a boatload of Indians from Jean Marie overtook and passed us, all of them waving and smiling. A bit later the chief's boat came along. We had a wistful thought, "perhaps he'll offer us a tow." But he too passed by.

One other boat we kept alert for never came: the one the Monus family used. When we left they were discussing the feasibility of coming to Fort Simpson for the Dominion Day Celebration, but they were expecting a barge to arrive that same day in Jean Marie, and their duty required them to stay for the unloading. This was our first experience with flexible scheduling on the Mackenzie. Although the barge was due on Friday, July 1, it might just as likely show up on Saturday, or Sunday, or maybe next week, wind and weather being what they were. Also, it was the first time we had seen how dependent the communities are on barges for their supplies. If a barge is too many days late, the people are on short rations in a hurry.

Brian and Lincoln chattered about the fun they'd had with their new Indian friends, and speculated over whether they would make any more friends at Fort Simpson. As the town grew nearer Linc started to ask where "Martini" was located. He insisted this was the name of a place we would reach before Fort Simpson and wanted to know if we would stop there. Nick, who knew better, argued with him for miles. Finally, in exasperation, he handed Linc the map and ordered him to show where in the world he had found such a place. Sure enough, there it was: "Martin I.," but in the hand lettering of the map the abbreviated form for "Martin Island" looked exactly like "Martini."

The author proudly holds a northern pike, caught with lightweight trout spinning gear on a Wob-l-rite lure, near Camsell Bend. The cabin in the background belongs to the Game Management Service and is regularly used by its employees in the line of work. It is kept padlocked when not in use.

Clothes smoke dry during a calm after a storm while Lincoln fishes for pike in the bright midsummer evening.

At Jean Marie Creek the Indians square logs in their cooperatively owned sawmill. This summer these were floated over a hundred miles north to aid in building the new town of Wrigley. The hard hats seem to be a status symbol among the men as well as safety headgear.

At Fort Simpson the Royal Canadian Mounted Police Officer, Corporal Berg, holds a four-month-old husky-malemute. This young man lives in a large comfortable RCMP residence with his wife and children. Most of the service families we met expressed deep affection for their isolated duty stations.

Mile after mile we paddled along, growing more tired but making excellent time. Even so it became obvious we would not arrive in time for any of the celebration, but we decided to keep on anyway. Seven hours out of Jean Marie we sighted the island on which Fort Simpson stands, and an hour later were crossing the Liard River where it enters the Mackenzie just above town. Such a muddy, debris-infested river was that Liard! It drains a watershed from the Yukon Territory, and carries in it almost enough silt to plow. The Liard and Mackenzie waters flow side by side over a hundred and fifty miles before they mix; the line of demarcation between them is startlingly clear.

Across the current we toiled. We flashed along the steep bank which edged the town, then spun into the back eddy formed by the Royal Canadian Mounted Police floating dock. We tied to the dock, and stepped out, as thirty or more people peered down at us from the cliff top. Then a young white man came walking down the long stretch of wooden steps from above and gave us greeting:

"Well, I see you made it. I've been looking for you. I saw you at the airport in Fort Smith, and listened in on your conversation. Are you enjoying your trip?"

Thus our formal meeting with Emile Gautreau, a young man of Acadian background who again showed us that incomparable Canadian hospitality. He had a brief consultation with Nick, and the two of them left while the rest of us stretched our legs and kept an eye on things. Interestingly enough, none of the Indians came down to the dock. It seemed to be "off limits." However, this was not so with the water. Several times a young Indian in a freight canoe, powered by at least a 28-horsepower motor, came surging by as close to where we were tied as he dared. He had a couple of young boys with him. They were having a great time trying to swamp our kayaks — of this I am convinced — judging from the way they cut and capered back and forth. But Devon and I pretended not to be worried as the kayaks wobbled away in the wash and wake. After a few passes the Indians gave up the game, much to our relief.

In just a little while Nick came striding down the stairs smiling a smile that said "good news." We had been wondering where we were to stay, and thanks to Emile's help, we now had a home. Emile introduced him to Sister Champagne of the Grey Nuns of Montreal who manage the large St. Margaret's Hospital at Fort Simpson. The Sister immediately offered the front lawn for a campsite, then showed my husband how to get to the shower and rest-room facilities in the hospital basement. Emile, meanwhile, went over to the local hotel which had the only restaurant in town. Normally dinner was served between six and seven, but it was now almost nine. When he returned dinner had been arranged. About this time a man in a fine-looking navy blue uniform walked up. For a moment we mistook him for the still missing Royal Canadian Mounted Police, but a second look identified him as our Mills Lake friend, Captain Nelson of the *Tembah*. Our greetings were cordial, we compared notes on weather and learned that he had met only balmy days, for the storm which had caused us all our trouble was so localized that it hadn't even extended fifty miles. Captain Nelson and the *Tembah* were sailing for Fort Norman at three in the morning, so we parted with great expectations of more reunions farther along the river.

We trudged up the steep stairways to the hospital lawn with a minimum of camping gear, deposited it, then walked down the board sidewalk one-half a block to the "Fort Simpson Hotel, Ltd., J. G. Kidd, Prop." The hotel dining room looked just like that of many a resort area in the Sierra of California. At one end of the room stood a shuffleboard table. At the opposite end was the juke box and a magazine rack which held every major U. S. publication plus a collection of the trashiest stuff imaginable. Nearby was a circular display of paperbacks, from good to garbage. Along the wall between the magazines and the shuffleboard stretched a long counter and the pass-through to the kitchen. The counter displayed what our department stores call "sundries," including a magnificent array of tobaccos and candy bars. Behind the counter was a huge coffee urn and a juice dispenser, a rack of eating utensils, a toaster, and paper napkins with a large sign announcing "serve yourself." The rest of the room was partly filled with tables and chairs, but a portion near the shuffleboard was clear, probably for dancing. The only thing missing was a bar and, although there were signs advertising soft drinks, there was no mention of beer. Fort Simpson, we were to learn, was a dry town.

Wearily we sat down at a large table to catch our breaths. The first move Nick made was to go over to the counter and buy himself a pack of cigarettes. The rest of us glowered at him, but he smiled contentedly and poured himself a cup of coffee from the coffee urn, drew another for me, and came back to the table. Serve yourselves," he told the boys.

"Oh boy," said the younger ones, and dashed for the juice dispenser. Devon followed to the coffee urn.

As we relaxed and sipped there were promising noises and smells coming from the kitchen. In a little while, J. G. Kidd himself appeared with delicious mushroom omelets for all, then brought a mug of coffee and joined us at the table.

Kidd, like Sieg Philipps, knew the Northwest Territories to be his land of opportunity. He had bought the hotel and brought his wife and children there to live. In addition to running the hotel and restaurant, he learned to bake and turned out all the bread for the town, the school, and the village of Jean Marie. Finally he had just been licensed by the government to run hunting and fishing parties to nearby areas, including the Nahani Valley and the Root River. These are fabulous areas for dahl sheep, moose, bear, caribou, and fish. All you need is time and money, an experienced outfitter can guarantee the rest. We listened, fascinated, as Kidd described his busy life.

Then we talked about our trip. Kidd was the first to mention a hazard ahead of us: the Sans Sault Rapids. "Keep to your left," he urged. "A man was drowned there a few years back when he went down the right side." Nick was instantly alert and started questioning him in detail. He had a map in his room, so he and Nick and Devon left to study it. But it was too far in the future for me to be bothered — far beyond Norman Wells, almost a month away — so I sat and wrote post cards home and people-watched.

Several oil workers, white men of middle age, came in and poured themselves some coffee. They were wearing work clothes, and looked like people from the U.S. A group of teen-agers, Indian youths and their dates, entered and started to feed the juke box. They too looked like boys and girls from the States, although their clothing was less conservative. The boys wore black pointed-toed low boots, tight-fitting pants, flashy jackets, and over-long hair. The girls wore stretch pants, color-ful blouses, beehive ratted hair-dos, and plenty of make-up. They were, I judged, about a year behind that summer's styling in the States, but it was easy to speculate on where they got their taste. I had to smile at them, for they reminded me so much of my students back home. They smiled back, and went over to the food counter to take care of that perpetual hunger universal among the teens.

We went back to the hospital grounds and put up our tents near the fences in a front corner of the lawn. Again we ob-served that there was a second "off limits" place for the towns-people: the hospital yard. We knew our belongings would be safe.

Now stretching ahead of us was an hour of joy: shower time! Quickly we gathered together clean clothes, soap, and our last two clean towels. Nick led the way around to the rear of the hospital, where we passed through what we called a "mosquito lock" – an outer door, a little hallway, and an inner door. Every public building and almost every private home in the Mackenzie has such arrangements. They really are designed for times of extreme cold, to keep cold out and warm in, but they serve a purpose during insect time too, so "mosquito locks" they were to us.

We tiptoed downstairs to the hospital basement, and there it was: a real shower! I can't tell you how good it felt to be clean again. Unless you've bathed with bucket baths and skinny dips for a couple of weeks you can only guess at the sensuous pleasure of a warm, soapy shower. It didn't matter that we could only damp-dry on our shared towels. What did count was we were clean! Clean! Clean! We gathered up our grimy clothes and floated back to our tents. I dumped the clothes in a

corner, said goodnight to the little boys, and stepped outside
to join Nick and Devon for a walk around town. The problem
of how to wash those clothes could be solved tomorrow, but
tonight we wanted to look at the town.

✓　　　　✓　　　　✓

I woke up at 8:00, ready to go, but the others seemed to be
in deep slumber so I left the tent quietly and went to the hospital basement. The laundry, the kitchen, and the refectory
were all in the basement too. As I was leaving the bathroom I
was greeted in the hallway by two nuns, Sister Lethiecq and
Sister Lemire. I remember one asking me if it felt good to be
"out of the bush" and the other remarking, "You came all the
way without a kicker?" I made a mental note to stop referring
to "brush" and "motors" while in this land.

Sister Lethiecq was about to go on duty, but Sister Lemire
invited me to have a cup of coffee. An hour later, while we
were deep in earnest conversation about some of the problems
of the youth of the Northwest Territories — the educational
needs, the moral standards, the problems of "nothing to do" —
the rest of my family came down. Introductions exchanged, we
excused ourselves and went to the hotel for breakfast. I remember remarking to my husband what a quick, keen mind the
Sister had. He replied, "She should have. You've been talking
to the Sister Superior. She's probably responsible for the whole
operation of the hospital."

We feasted that morning, because Brian and Devon the day
before had each caught a fish. They had cleaned them, wrapped
them, and left them in our kayaks. Now we brought them up
to Mrs. Kidd with the bargain to keep one for her family and
cook one for breakfast. The feature of the meal, however, was
the vast quantity of hot-buttered toast we all devoured. After
ten days of baking powder biscuits, corn bread, and pancakes,
I felt I could eat a roomful of toast, a feeling matched by the
whole family.

Next we faced a delightful chore: picking up our mail. We
gave the younger boys their freedom and a dollar each, told
them we would see them in a while at the Hudson's Bay store,

and went to the post office. A great stack of letters awaited us, half for Devon from the Girl Back Home, and half for us from friends and relations.

Our next chore was a shopping trip at Hudson's Bay, that historic chain of trading posts founded in 1620, now up-dated and stylishly, even officially, known as the "Bay." This trading post looked like a small, modern U. S. supermarket. On display in front was a fiberglassed speedboat, big enough for a forty horsepower kicker. Inside, the store was one-third grocery, and two-thirds everything else. The only competitor in town was a small free trader at the river's edge, therefore, as you might imagine, trading was brisk. We did some stocking up at the Bay, replenishing our supply of coffee, bacon, soap and repellent, adding a few candy bars, buying enough food to see us through the day's lunch and our first dinner on the river, and choosing the hats we had foolishly neglected to buy in the States. Nick, Devon, and Linc carried our supplies to camp while I made our next call.

Back home, our friend (Luther) Duc Meyer had told us about Bompas Hall, the dormitory (called "hostel" in the Northwest) for Anglican and other Protestant children who must board when they come to school. He said to be sure to look up Mrs. Jean Lawson, the matron of the hostel, so I was on my way to introduce myself. What he had not told me and what I was too dense to figure out was that he had written Jean to tell her we were coming. I stood in the hallway rehearsing a carefully-planned little speech when a tiny grey-haired lady, moving as briskly as if propelled by a tightly-wound spring, came to me and inquired, "How do you do?"

"My name is Elinor Nickerson. . . ." I started.

"I'm so glad to meet you. I'm Jean Lawson. I've been expecting you."

Her handshake was hearty. Her voice merry. Her pleasure genuine.

"How is Duc?" she asked.

When I told her he was on his way north and would be along within the month, again there was joy. Jean was about to leave for her two-week vacation Outside. Indeed, her plane was

due out at 3:30 that afternoon. We had three hours ahead in
which to do a lot of visiting, so we got right down to it. Brian
was sent to bring back Nick and the laundry; Jean's first
thought was "You'll want to do a wash." Then we made a tour
of the hostel.

Those hostels in the three school centers of the Northwest
Territories (Yellowknife, Fort Simpson, and Inuvik) are really
amazing. Designed to care for hundreds of children who are
brought in from the surrounding countryside, financed by the
government, they are provisioned to withstand a siege. In the
deep cellars there is storage room for almost the entire school
year's food supply which is brought in by barge in late summer. The hot water supply tank is monstrous, and a source of
great pride, not to say comfort. Each student receives one new
set of clothes, head to toe, and one old set, neatly mended and
clean. As a regular daily practice fresh underwear and socks
are issued to every child each morning. The shower rooms are
immense and, Jean assured me, very popular. She had expected
resistance from the children, particularly those natives who live
in the bush during the summer and never see a bath from mid-
May to early September. "But they take to the water like
ducks" — her words — and shower time is a highlight of the day
for them. (Nick had remarked only the night before that it only
takes a couple of weeks of living without hot running water to
find how much you take it for granted.) The last of our tour
showed us the sleeping rooms for the children, the staff apart-
ments, the common rooms and, finally, the kitchen.

Nick and Devon appeared, and now ensued three memorable hours. In the kitchen, seated at a large table, were Mr.
Otto Kufeldt, administrator of the Protestant school; Mrs. An-
nette Sey, girls' counselor, and her small daughter, Muriel; Bruce
Sawula, boys' counselor; and the reverend Mr. George Hamilton, pastor of the Anglican Church. For three hours we sat and
talked, drinking gallons of tea, and settling every educational
and sociological problem in the Northwest Territories. From
time to time I would step down the hall to the laundry room
where our modest pile of clothes was being lashed clean by the
school's huge commercial-sized washers and dryers. By the time

they were finished I knew I had mastered one more skill to
tide me over in my old age: I could probably run a small commercial laundry.

The afternoon raced by. Muriel forgot her shyness and went
off to play with Brian and Linc. We found that the Mackenzie
had problems that were far more like ours back home than different from them. And at last it was time for Mrs. Lawson's
plane. We said our goodbyes to Jean, wishing her a good holiday Outside, arranged to meet Mr. Hamilton for dinner, and
went back to our tent to put away our clean laundry.

Just as I finished, a woman and a young girl approached
and introduced themselves. Although the older woman was not
an Indian, she "looked Indian," and the girl with her was at
least part Indian. We invited them to enter the tent, and we all
sat — on the floor, of course. This was how we met Mrs. Alphon-
sine Cazon, the wife of the chief of the Indians at Fort Simpson,
and one of her daughters. Mrs. Cazon had heard of our arrival
and had brought a pair of men's mukluks in the hope of selling
them to Devon. She had made them for her son, she said, but
he preferred the white man's footwear. Oddly enough it was
not our son who fell in love with those beautifully hand-crafted
soft boots, but Nick. Mrs. Cazon made an on-the-spot sale, plus
two more orders for Brian and Lincoln. We had a delightful
visit with her, and parted after exchanging addresses in hopes
of further business dealings.

Our next visitor was Miss Maureen Woodward, a registered
nurse at St. Margaret's. Maureen was just off duty from work,
and having heard of our arrival, she had come to invite us for
coffee that evening, to a little party around 9:30. We consulted
our rapidly-filling social calendar and decided that the Reverend Mr. Hamilton would probably appreciate seeing us leave
early inasmuch as next day was Sunday, and accepted with
pleasure. Then we left the tent and took our cameras for a
picture-taking tour of Fort Simpson.

It's a mighty busy place, Fort Simpson. The population
numbers around 850, not counting several hundred school children who live at the two hostels (one Anglican, one Roman
Catholic) during the school year. The government conducts

an experimental farm at the edge of town. The hospital serves
the territory from Norman Wells to Yellowknife. No road
reaches as far as Simpson, but an all-year airport located just
a short way from town, and a snye for floatplanes made where
a creek enters the river, keep the people in flying touch with
the world. Although vehicular traffic is light by our standards,
the fort has stop signs and yield signs at strategic intersections
and several one-way streets. There is a large community recreation hall, and a theater which shows nightly movies. Fort
Simpson clearly expects to grow.

We met the reverend Mr. Hamilton and went with him to
the hotel for a very satisfactory dinner. During the evening we
learned that the priest had spent most of his ministry in the Far
North. Now he and his wife (who was visiting Outside with
their children) were preparing to leave for their next post, in
the Bahamas. "What a change from the frozen North!" we exclaimed, but Mr. Hamilton was facing it much more calmly.

"I'll go where they send me," he said, and that was about
the sum of his comments on the Bahamas.

When we left our friend we returned to camp speculating
on the nature of the party to which we had been invited.
Would it really be coffee and cookies? Or home-brew and
crackers? During the day we had heard several references to
a typical "Far North party" that was being thrown that night,
and we wondered if Maureen had merely been using a euphe-
mism for a binge. We decided that were it the latter we would
go lightly. Just in case, we sent the younger boys off to the
movies, then we joined Maureen at the hospital gate and went
with her to the coffee party.

And it was just that, to our genuine relief and pleasure. For
two hours we visited with Maureen and her friend, Mrs. Susan
Lindberg, over coffee and home-made cookies. Susan's husband
owns a small tugboat and pushes barges between Fort Simpson
and Yellowknife all summer long. They live on the barge, and
Susan says they love it. We had waved at a small tug which
passed us on our way from Jean Marie. I pronounced to the
family that there was a woman on board because of the nature
of the wash flying on lines stretched across the deck. It was,

indeed, an accurate pronouncement, for Susan herself had been one of the people who waved back. I don't remember asking her what they did in the winter, but I believe they lived at Fort Simpson, another young couple who called the Far North "home". Maureen, on the other hand, was a wayfarer, a nurse contracted to St. Margaret's for two years. At the end of this time she planned to marry and settle down on a ranch in Montana.

With such pleasantries, such exchanges of autobiographical information, we passed the evening until at eleven we said goodnight and started walking back to the tent. It occurred to me then that we had made no arrangements to meet the younger boys after the show. I wondered if they yet knew their way around, if there were a curfew, if we would have to bail them out of the Canadian equivalent of "Juvies". No need to fuss—they were sound asleep in their down sleeping bags, surrounded by stacks of new horror comics. Remembering my years of poring over the Sunday supplement's "Secrets of the French Sûreté" I tried not to shudder over their choice in comic books. It was nice to find them home safe: they were really growing up.

The next morning I was in the hospital basement by 7:45, hoping that Sister Lemire's schedule would have her finishing breakfast at the same time and that perhaps we would be able to continue our conversation of the previous morning. Luck was with me, and apparently the Sister's interest coincided with mine. Soon we were seated over coffee at the refectory table, and before long had launched into a discussion of world politics. The springboard to this new talk was her question: "What brings you to the Mackenzie?" and my answer, "Escape. We are running away, for a time. Our world will be there when we get back."

Nick appeared and the three of us sat together. At the Sister's invitation coffee expanded to toast and marmalade and cheese and fruit. We moved from the refectory to her office on the main floor, and the good conversation flowed between us. I remember saying to her, "You must enjoy the summer season when the tourists come by and visit."

"Well," said Sister Lemire, "they don't pay attention to the nuns," and I thought, "more fools they . . ."

Finally, of course, it was time to leave. We said our farewells at the hospital steps with Sister cautioning us to take care and wishing us God Speed. I was to hear her name mentioned with respect and affection by many people all down the river. I felt we had been privileged to share so much of her busy day.

In another hour we would be on the river again. One more person remained who had to be contacted: The Royal Canadian Mounted Policeman who, so far, had eluded us. Now we went across the street and met, finally, Corporal Berg, the young Mountie who had been so busy keeping law and order over Dominion Day that he had managed only two hours sleep in the past forty-eight! We had noticed a goodly bit of coming and going around the jail house, but did not have time to snoop. Apparently a few people had gotten drunk on home brew, and Corporal Berg had his work cut out for him. We met him in time to say goodbye, and to give him our estimated time of arrival at Fort Norman, three hundred and thirty-four miles distant, the location of the next R.C.M.P. detachment.

Maureen was waiting at the stairs to the dock to take our pictures. Sister Lethiecq, who had spent much time traveling by kayak as a young woman, was waiting too. Townspeople returning from church gathered to see us off. They all wished us good luck. The magic of the river awaited us, and we launched smoothly into the calm, swift stream.

"I wonder what happened to Emile Gautreau," Nick said. "I haven't seen him since the first night."

Sure enough, we had lost track of our first benefactor without even the chance to thank him properly. We wondered if we would ever see him again.

8 «
NEW FORT WRIGLEY

The morning we left Fort Simpson we moved in an absolute calm, with not even a zephyr stirring the water. Enchanted, we leaned on our paddles and listened to the town as we glided on the swift current. Passing by the powerhouse we heard the generators hum. The voices of people drifted across the water. We heard dogs barking, babies crying, a power saw, a carpenter hammering. We left the point of the island, but the sounds, though fading, lingered. Then as they receded a new sound intruded on our consciousness: the buzzing of tiny insect wings. We had been overtaken by a new kind of pest: bulldog flies.

These things look like oversized deerflies, and that's what we called them until we reached Norman Wells and a resident renamed them for us. They paced us as we paddled along, diving over and about in a sort of figure eight, sometimes landing, but generally just buzzing us like kamikazes. If we speeded up, they speeded up. If we let the current carry us, they slowed down. More and more flies joined up until we felt as if we were being herded down the river. It was maddening.

I took a swipe at one of them and by chance made contact. With a satisfying "thunk" the nasty thing flipped into the water and lay there struggling on its back. Brian reached over with his paddle and quietly shoved the fly under. By this time Nick and Linc and Devon were swinging their paddles too. Thus we invented a new game, "Deer Fly Lacrosse," a game with no rules and only a score: whoever "thunked" the most was champion. The game lasted until we ran out of flies or calm, and proved a really effective way to Pollyanna a pesky situation. Later, in talking to local residents, we were told they had never run into this sort of thing: traveling by motorboat they simply outran the insects.

We went twenty miles that day, crossed over to the clear side of the river, and camped on a sandbank. Devon found a spot where Arctic grayling were biting, and caught our breakfast fish. After our whirlwind social life in town we were glad to be back on the river, and turned in early that night to catch up on sleep.

Next day was Fourth of July. We flew the stars and stripes on the little eighteen-inch flag mast at the bow of Nick's boat, and fired salutes with the heavy rifle, but the real fireworks were supplied by the weather. All morning long the weather worsened, and by lunchtime ominous black clouds were threatening on the west, and thunder muttered from behind them. We know that thunder means lightning and lightning means "get off the river," so we made for the east shore. We edged along just a few feet from the bank for as long as we dared, then pulled in to an extremely rocky shore and secured the boats. There we sat in our waterproof parkas and watched the rain and lightning draw nearer and nearer until we thought both would surely hit us, but this was not our day to become casualties of lightning. Accompanied by marvelous blasts of thunder, it only bounced about us and moved on. The rain was moderate and quite warm.

When I was sure that we were not doomed this time, I started in on my favorite camping activity: building a good campfire. After some food we went back to our boats with the idea of doing another ten miles. I had taken off my boat boots and was riding barefoot when I gradually became aware of the fact that my feet were wet. Those rocks! We had torn open a hole in the boat.

"Leak," I screeched. "Hey, anybody."

But they were all far out of earshot. Brian looked around at me from the comic book he was reading. "Whatsamatter?" he asked.

"Leak! Get the whistle! Hurry!"

"Okay," he said and scrabbled about in the bilge.

Theoretically each person had a police whistle for use in emergency, but actually only each boat had one. Once in awhile all three mysteriously landed in one boat and I was praying that this was the day at least one whistle was in our boat. We learned long ago that we never stay together on our kayak trips. Probably we should, and now and then we do, but what with one person taking pictures, another doing laundry over the side, and a third paddling vigorously, we sometimes get spread out for a couple of miles. It is a grand way to get a feeling of isolation—to commune alone with the silences of the great river—or even to work out a grouch if it is that sort of day, without imposing on your companions, but with a leak in the boat, companionship is needed in a hurry.

In the past we had worried ourselves a bit by this tendency to stray, so we bought three walkie-talkies, one for each boat, with the idea that we could keep track of ourselves better. Each transceiver had the grandest printed commercial in its fabric-lined box, calling it a "Fine piece of electronic equipment" but warning "like all equipment of this type the operating range depends upon varying terrain and conditions." Under conditions described as "favorable, over water" the range was said to be four or five miles. We soon found this to be the purest hogwash: the range was just about a mile. But it was better talking by radio than shouting over water, although often it sounded as if we were talking in an echo chamber when the sender's voice came drifting across the water moments after being received by radio!

At last we established contact with Nick and Devon who were just abeam of a beautiful little sand and gravel beach. Even though we had only come ten miles, we decided to make camp. Nick got to work patching the boat, Devon soon had the fishing gear out and brought in two pike to supplement our dinner. As we finished eating we heard in the distance the unmistakable throbbing of Diesel engines. Soon a large tug pushing a tremendous string of barges came into sight, going north. We stood on the shore staring through our binoculars and were amused to see at least three of the crew standing on deck staring right back at us through binoculars too. We never tired of watching the river traffic, and were particularly charmed by the tugs and barges. It looked like a grand way to spend a summer, combining work and adventure and leisure in sensible proportions. Soon the tug was gone, with a toot on the whistle and much waving from us and the crew, the wake finally reached shore and washed against the sides of our beached boats. My log book reads, "Tuesday, 5th, poured last night for a couple of hours, a.m. promises a gorgeous day. We have sighted mountains."

The mountain sighting came about as a result of Devon's growing restlessness to see something other than flat terrain. The map indicated mountains to the northwest, but so far we could not see them. Devon decided to climb the high bank behind our camp for a scouting look. First he had to put on his bush armor: lined pants, boots, sweatshirt, rubberized parka, gloves, headnet, and repellent. By this time we all wanted to go along, so we all had to put on armor. In case of bears Devon carried the rifle, Nick and I had cameras and the boys walked free. Straight up the bank we clawed, about 45 feet, and then we turned and looked. Sure enough, in a pale blue line across the river we could see the first mountains, two days distant by kayak. We skidded down the bank on the seats of our pants, and shoved off for a long, long day. We did not find a suitable place to stop until six o'clock that night.

You might think that, with hundreds of miles of untouched shoreline to choose from, finding a campsite would be the easiest thing in the world. Well, it just isn't so. Naturally, in an emergency you can haul into shore almost anywhere and make do, but normally you don't elect to stay in a "make do" site. Many things enter into site selection: beaching the boats for one thing. Counting our weight each double kayak carries over a quarter of a ton, therefore we prefer a beach landing where the boats can be unloaded and then lifted onto shore. It is not safe to let them ride in the water all night. Dragging them on shore before unloading can cause leaks, such as the one just mended in my boat.

A good campsite also needs a nice, flat place for a tent. You'd be surprised how hard these are to come by. Then there should be a good kitchen area. I hate cooking on the sand; I love cooking among gravel and boulders. The reasons should be obvious, unless you like the crunch of grit in your food.

Finally there is the question of water. Of course, you can always use the river water. Early in the trip this was the thing to do. But from Fort Simpson on, after the entrance of the muddy Liard, the water is less attractive, and as the water muddies, the fishing (angling) drops off to nothing. Where a creek or stream or river joins the Mackenzie you find more potable water and fish again.

So we fuss-pot about our camping sites, and sometimes we go a lot more miles than our muscles would like before finally exclaiming, "This is the place."

That night was one of our "Camp Desperation" type camps: up on a mudbank, with mosquito-ridden grass for the tent, sand for the kitchen, and muddy water for human consumption (we were on the Liard side of the river). The one redeeming factor was a huge pile of driftwood for fire near the spot where I would be cooking.

As we settled in we were entertained by the frantic behavior of two full-grown seagulls. We have observed these birds on other trips, and our conclusion is that they show some of the stupidest behavior of any bird ever. The moment you approach within a half-mile of a seagull's nesting place, one or two adult birds will come zooming out to you and start squawking at you to go away. This ridiculous display is a sure cue to follow if you want to observe baby gulls. We judged from the hysterics of the gulls around our camp that there must have been a nest very close by. Each time we went for wood the birds dove so close to us that we thought they were going to hit us. Finally, in the morning, Lincoln went on a careful search around the pile of driftwood. With the two guarding gulls almost colliding in the air he found the object of their concern: a tiny fuzzy grey and black-spotted baby bird. He blended so closely with his hiding place that each of us had to be shown in turn. He never stirred, never even blinked an eye as we peered in at him. After getting a good look and taking a picture we stayed away from the woodpile, but the two guardians took turns diving and screaming at us. When we broke camp they followed us for a quarter of a mile before leaving.

White picket fences and a Cape Cod feeling awaited us at Wrigley Airport. Left to right: Lincoln, Devon, the author, and Brian.

The challenge of constructing a town for fifty families, under primitive working conditions, with partially trained labor, and in a space of two to three months was met here at Fort Wrigley's new site. Devon looks at a generator which was put in service only a day or two before we arrived. 'Round the clock crews worked in the 24 hours of mid-summer daylight.

The fine art of camp cookery as exemplified by stew and dumplings, made from dried and dehydrated products.

Devon drifts and dreams in the Arctic summer twilight. The absolute stillness of mid-stream during such a calm cannot be duplicated even in our favorite vacation spots back home. This was the year our younger sons finally learned to enjoy "listening" to the quiet.

A couple of hours later we saw what appeared to be a dock site, so we went ashore. We found we had landed at an abandoned oil exploration camp. For the next hour we snooped and explored and surmised and, in our imaginations, reconstructed the operation. A road led to the top of a high bluff, where, spread out before us was the camp proper. Behind us a wide swath in the trees ran in a beeline over the hills and out of sight. Another stretched out in a different direction, and still another in a third direction. We learned later that this is the pattern of oil exploration. A camp is set up, and straight lines are cleared for mile after mile. At certain intervals test drills are made. Whether or not anyone has really hit paying oil we do not know. We do know that at the present time Norman Wells is the only operating oil field in the entire Mackenzie District, and that several major oil companies are spending many thousands of dollars all year 'round in oil exploration.

Now we were entering the mountains, approaching the entrance of the Nahani River on the west. We made camp on the east side of the river, with a black sky threatening, but after a little sprinkle the storm did not materialize. We were just finishing dinner when we saw a strange sight: far on the river behind us, in midstream, a raft appeared. As it drew nearer we could see that it was made of many logs, perhaps sixty feet long and twenty feet wide, and in the center was a kind of lean-to tent. Tied on behind was a scow with two kickers. Four men were on the raft, lying about on the deck taking their ease. We recognized this as a shipment of logs from Jean Marie on the way to be delivered at the new Fort Wrigley site. We waved and they waved, and so to bed.

Next day the paddling was wonderful, the day calm and bright. The current picked up, and the sky filled with cloud formations of such spectacular quality that Duc Meyer later described them as "Rorschachs in the sky." Brian kept exclaiming over the scenery and mourning because his camera was not capable of catching the ever-changing shadows on the mountains. That night we came to the cabin of the "Canadian Game Management" and, for a change, pitched our tents on the deep moss of its front yard. The cabin, though padlocked, still offered the shelter of a large porch. There was even a table on which I set up cooking, using the Optimus stove. Here we settled for two nights, partly to rest and partly because it was raining. We were high on a bluff overlooking the water, down through an avenue of trees, at the spot on the river known as Camsell Bend, said by some to be the most beautiful scenery on the whole Mackenzie.

There we were entertained by the antics of a small mouse which scurried among the crumbs. The mosquitoes were out in full force, and for the first time we encountered the tiny biters known as "No-see-ums." These quite easily get through the screen, but increased application of repellent discouraged most of them. Another noise we heard once in awhile was a little harder to identify. Nick and Devon decided it sounded like a moose, and it really was possible to imagine a moose emitting that sort of a sound. The only catch was I thought it sounded exactly like a noise we had heard up in the Sierra the previous summer. There we had called it an "escaped burro" so as not to alarm the people with us, though we really suspected it was a bear. I didn't choose to argue with the men. In fact, I just did not want to think about it at all because I am afraid of bears. But I wrote in my log, "Oh well, if we're here tomorrow, it's probably a moose."

We passed the long hours of the day in idleness. Each of us had a deck of cards and lots of reading material. We also had a booklet of New York *Times* Crossword Puzzles, and this provided the main activity of the day. Never have I had so much fun sharing in a crossword puzzle! The tent jumped with our raucous laughter as we invented words and finally deduced the correct ones. We even finished one puzzle!

Four times during the day we had visitors. The first was a boat traveling north with two geologists who were heading for Inuvik. A little later the scow with the four Jean-Marie-Creek Indians came by. When they stopped we brewed some coffee and visited for awhile. The men, who had been riding the log raft, said they felt like heroes at new Fort Wrigley, because the project had run out of timber and men were about to be laid off when they arrived. They were now on their way home to pick up another raft. Our next visitors were a game management man, his wife, and their two children, who arrived in a speedboat. They were in a big hurry, so their visit with us was extremely offhand. They bustled up the slope to the cabin, opened it up and threw together a dinner out of cans, gobbled it down, then dashed on their way. Just before leaving, the man mentioned that a scow with eight of his crew was due —they were all on the way to a fire, or something. Sure enough the crew arrived. They pulled in to shore, built a great fire to serve both for cooking and warmth, and proceeded to broil about three dozen pork chops. Each man ate his share, climbed back on the boat, and took off. The meat constituted their entire meal. Before they left they told us our "moose" sound had probably been made by a mother bear and two cubs.

We stood by their fire and talked for awhile; then the rain came again and drove us to our tents, early to bed. All night it stormed, but by morning the weather let up to the point where we were on our way again. For twenty miles we played tag with wet, weeping clouds until at last we agreed it was time to stop, and beached at a likely spot. Only one thing bothered us: there was almost, but not quite, a place for the big tent.

Just as we were getting ready to move on I remembered a camping trick from my Chaparral days. We used to level sleeping spaces among the redwoods by excavating the duff here and filling it there, using fallen logs for retainers. By placing several different driftwood logs on the down slope of the beach and shoveling out a bit of the up slope we could have a tent space in a very short time, I suggested. Nick and Dev liked the idea, and in five minutes had excavated and filled a perfect spot. From then on we had to do at least a little shoveling for every campsite, like all proper real-estate developers. In five more minutes both tents were up and we turned toward unloading the boats. Then Dev, who had paused to look over the scene, let out a yell,

"Run for cover! Here it comes!"

All unnoticed, a monstrous black cloud with a huge sheet of water hanging down from it had sneaked over the hills rising on the beach above our camp and at that very moment was drenching the stand of trees about fifty yards away. We had mistaken the sound of rain for the rustle of wind in the leaves. Every bucket in the sky poured down on us. The Indians say that in this part of the country, "The mountains make the weather." We were ready, at last, to believe it.

There we sat in the tent, with all of our supplies in the boats, including our rain gear. Who's going to get sopped? How long will this go on? When will I ever be able to fix dinner in this downpour? Worry, worry, worry! But in twenty minutes the shower had stopped. Good luck still rode with us.

While the others carried gear from the kayaks, I went about the woman's work of locating the kitchen and bringing in the initial firewood. It is said that you can find dry wood and tinder under fallen logs. I am happy to report that this is true even when the rest of your family stands around deploring, "Where will we ever get any dry wood?" Then the trick is to get a fire hot enough to dry out any wet wood placed on it, and finally to get a roarer going that even the rain won't damp down. These bonfires are a dividend of camping where there is lots of driftwood and no fire hazard.

All night long it stormed. I woke several times, and lay there reveling in the excitement of the thunder, wind, lightning, and rain. The darkness was still only a twilight, and I could see much of the river and mountains by just turning my head. It was hard to tell sometimes where dreaming left off and storm-watching began. By morning it became obvious that the storm had not yet blown over, so being restless, I left the tent and walked down to the beach for a closer look at the boats. What a shock! We had hauled them up on the sandbank, but during the storm the waves had undercut the bank. Each boat was in immediate peril of sliding into the river. A few quick lifts and tugs and hauls at bow and stern and all was made safe. Feeling very smug I resolved to henpeck the men about their careless boat beaching and went back to bed. At noon camp showed signs of waking, so the cook prepared brunch. By late afternoon the river was glassy and the sky superb, so we paddled for 25 miles on mirror-smooth water. Several times we were passed by motorboats, and once by the

Tembah, going upstream. By the next day, Tuesday, July 12th, we were in sight of the Franklin Mountains and keeping watch for the first signs of Wrigley Airport. About a mile before the airport we finally recognized a sound we had first identified as a boat: it was a generator. Sure enough, soon we saw a rude landing, and a bulldozed road leading away up the three-hundred foot banks. Our maps indicated an airport up there, so we tied the boats and climbed out to have a look.

You get the strangest feeling when you first see an airport of this kind. It is such a combination of primitive and modern that your emotions are stirred in at least two directions at once. The field was a smooth, graveled strip, set down in a sea of colorful wild flowers. Far across the field stood the radio towers and the seven or eight structures which housed the staff who operated the place: stark white with bright red trim, they looked as comfortable and civilized as if they were on Cape Cod. But nothing but bush country stretched in any direction for hundreds of miles, and their only contact with Outside was by radio, water, or air. Isolated but not isolated—what a fascinating place to live!

There were at least four residences, and several children played in the picket-fenced yards. We walked along a board sidewalk to the home of Mr. Ito, the communications man, and were immediately invited in for punch. There in the living room sat a familiar figure: Emile Gautreau, our friend from Fort Simpson. What a reunion! With him were two other men, one a bush pilot named Bob Cameron. Now we learned a little more about Gautreau. He is an entomologist, employed by the Canadian government. Summertime he spends in the bush, flying from place to place on business requiring his special knowledge. (This summer it was a blight attacking spruce trees.) In winter he has a desk job, "inside, where it's warm." He believes he lives in the best of two worlds.

While we were visiting and drinking punch, Mrs. Ito was busy in the kitchen. My cook's nose told me that dinner preparations were under way when we first arrived, and I could picture any housewife's dismay at the thought of five unexpected (not to mention uninvited) guests for dinner. So I made secret signals to Nick who quickly caught the gist, and we steered toward the door after about fifteen minutes' visit. Emile and his associate walked with us to the boats, and we said our final goodbyes. His work did not take him farther north, so we were not to meet again.

Half an hour later we reached our goal for the day, a beach near the site of the new village of Fort Wrigley. The first sound we heard was the generator, and the first interesting sight the remnants of a stack of squared timbers which had floated so many miles from Jean Marie Creek. Nick and Devon were anxious to case the village, so they did all their chores, and then started asking around for estimates of "how long before dinner?" Now I get anxious too, but there are some jobs which, once begun, can't easily be set aside. The beef stew was half prepared, and had about thirty minutes to go. Feeling magnanimous about staying behind, I told them "twenty minutes." Apologetically they took off for a little stroll, just "to see where the town is located" and "We'll be back right away." I suggested they take a walkie-talkie, but "No, we'll be right back."

They really meant it, every word, but they didn't come right back at all. I planned to give them twenty extra minutes of grace anyway and cleverly timed the dinner to come out just right, so I waited a half-hour before putting in the dumplings. I set out the dishes and utensils, then checked my watch. The dumplings were done, but where were the men? Grumbling, I served the younger boys their dinner. "If they can't get here on time they can eat soggy dumplings for all I care," I muttered. But I did care. Camp cookery is an art, and dumplings on top of dehydrated stew makes for *haute cuisine*. Such is too good for the likes of inconsiderate menfolk!

"Why didn't they take a radio?" I mumbled. I wished I had a cup of coffee, but we had used our last for breakfast and no more could be purchased until Old Fort Wrigley, seven miles on our way tomorrow. I stared up the path where they had gone, then stomped back to the tent. Angrily I ate a few bites of warmish stew and gluey dumplings. Brian and Lincoln, who are already wise to the ways of outraged womanhood, made no comment but kept their attention on their comic books.

An hour and a half after leaving on their twenty-minute walk, Nick and Dev came bouncing into camp. They knew they were in the doghouse, but they had seen such interesting sights that they thought it was worth it. Nick took over the job of mollifying Mommy while Dev served up the unappetizing glop which passed for dinner. I was being revoltingly polite in my replies to Nick's enthusiastic descriptions of what he had seen. His explanations were just so many words, words, words. It seems they reached the village site, a good three-quarters of a mile distant and up a hillside just as the assistant foreman was leaving the mess hall. He was so tickled to have visitors to his project that he had to give them the de luxe tour at once. All Nick's protests that his wife was waiting were brushed away: a man's man thinks nothing of the body in the kitchen. The tour had to be given now. And it sounded fascinating, but I was plenty sore. Finally Nick said the magic words—

"And he wants us to come back for coffee, and he'll take us on the whole tour again."

Later, about 10:00 p.m., seated in the log-house kitchen of the construction camp, I had to smile as I looked about the room. Dev had elected to stay behind and write letters, but Brian and Linc were deep in a stack of some of the camp literature: comic books. Nick and Mr. Bourke (the assistant foreman) and Fred Bower (the cook) were talking Man Talk about the beauty of the country and the wildness of the territories. Mr. Bourke, warming to his theme, finally stated, "I know how you and the boys must be enjoying this trip, but how does your wife ever stand it?"

"Don't worry about her," said Nick, "she's rugged!" And he meant it as the greatest of compliments.

I smiled, graciously I hope, and poured myself another "cuppa". There is nothing like a good mug of strong, black coffee, I thought, and wondered why I'd ever had my back up so high earlier in the evening. I resolved then and there that henceforth I would save my annoyances for something more important than fallen dumplings, and every now and then I remembered to keep that resolution.

9 «

NORMAN WELLS

At the time we visited the townsite of New Fort Wrigley actual construction had been going on for about five weeks. Uninformed as we were about this country, we were beginning to see some of the impact of modern society on Indian culture. This experiment in social welfare, moving an entire village from a very old site to a very new one, was most interesting. Many months and probably many years had been spent in planning. Some buildings were to be moved by barge from the old town, but most of the houses would be new. All the current knowledge of combatting cold and permafrost was being used in both design and construction. Ambitious ideas for more modern water supply and sanitation were also included, as were projects for a new nursing station and a new schoolhouse.

The reasons for the new town seemed logical to us, both when we heard them from Mr. Bourke and when, later, we visited with the schoolmaster and his wife in the old town. Wrigley is located on the west side of the river, the muddy Liard side. The water, while drinkable, looks most unappetizing, and any attempt at cleanliness is at least partly defeated by the quantity of silt in the washing. This same water, when frozen, is gradually destroying the town. Each spring during break-up the ice gouges away more and more of the site because of its location. Some of the houses are now only a few feet from the edge of the bank, about thirty feet above the river. One good chunk of ice could wipe them out in moments.

I gather that one condition of life in the Northwest Territories is to be ready to defer to the river. During spring break-up if it threatens your house, you move your house; you do not change the river. This time, the plan is to move the whole town to a relatively unthreatened new site instead of backing away a handful of homes a few more feet from the edge of the old town.

The action involves both education and self help. The Jean Marie Band is selling its lumber to the Canadian Department of Public Works. The DPW, which only this summer absorbed the Department of Indian Affairs, has hired white men and Indians for the job, the former to teach and lead, the latter to learn and eventually, it is sincerely hoped, to take over. In this particular project we are talking of a town population of, perhaps, fifty families.

We were astonished at what had been accomplished, but when we learned that crews were working twenty-four hours a day, taking complete advantage of the nearly-nightless season, it was easier to understand. First a large area had been cleared in what was to become the center of the town's business section. One of the model houses was quickly built and its kitchen and living room turned temporarily into a mess hall for the men. The three bedrooms housed the cook, the foreman, and the assistant foreman. Near the mess hall were large tents for some of the laborers. As far as I could determine, the white workers lived on the site in these temporary shelters. The Indians either camped on the beach in similar tents or commuted from the old townsite by motorboat. The mess hall seemed to be for everyone.

In laying out the town, wide streets and spacious lots had been bulldozed among the trees, mostly spruce and aspen. A road had already been punched across the hills, beeline, to the airport two miles upstream, so air freight was easy to deliver. River-barge freight was reached by another crude road which zigzagged down the slope, and brought up to camp from the river by a large sledge pulled by a tractor. A telephone line ran from the mess hall; you could pick up the receiver and dial Edmonton, 1200 miles distant, a local call! Of course there was radio communication too, through the airport services. A new generator hummed away, day and night. The cook's dearest new possession was a huge walk-in deepfreeze, standing unsheltered at the end of the central town square.

Many permanent buildings were well along in construction, a second completed one being a big warehouse which was already jammed to the rafters with building supplies. At the finish of the project this warehouse was slated to become a garage, and most of the downtown activities were planned for this area.

Sometimes the foreman sounded optimistic, and sometimes pessimistic. We really couldn't tell. But he was extremely proud of his work. The target date for completing construction to the point where the move could be started was freeze-up in October.

We walked around the new town and looked and listened and asked questions and marveled and wished we could return in a year to see for ourselves. It is, I believe, unfortunate that more people do not know about this experiment. We may well have been the only tourists to drop in on the project that summer.

After our tour and picture-taking we went over to the mess hall where, as guests of the cook, we had a feast of bacon, fresh eggs, pancakes, fruit juices, genuine maple syrup, hot chocolate, and coffee. They really do themselves well in these isolated construction camps where eating is concerned! With another gesture of Canadian hospitality Mr. Bower, the cook, sent us on our way with a slab of bacon and two dozen fresh eggs.

In a little more than an hour we paddled the seven-mile distance to Fort Wrigley, situated directly across the stream from a towering mass of rock which is identified on the map as "La Roch Qui Trempe à l'eau," or "The rock which soaks (its feet) in the water." This was a name which had completely charmed my husband when going over the maps back home and later, in talking to the schoolmaster, he referred to the rock by its French name. The schoolmaster replied,

"Oh, I've often wondered about that rock and if it had another name. Around here it's called 'Wrigley Rock'."

Here we walked to the Hudson's Bay store to pick up our mail and buy a few things, such as coffee, and a canned dinner, and treats to keep us until the next town, Fort Norman. To our disappointment the manager of the store said that no mail had arrived for us. I was skeptical, for he had not even looked at the stack of letters in front of him, but I assumed that in an outpost of this size letters from the States to strangers would not easily be overlooked. Nick must have been surprised too, for he was careful to tell the man our names and that we planned to stay several days at Norman Wells where we could pick up any chance mail if he would forward it.

We then left "the Bay" and walked down the street to the schoolmaster's house. There we met Mr. Patrick O'Leary and his wife who immediately asked us in for tea. We had heard of the O'Learys from Corporal Berg, the Royal Canadian Mounted Policeman in Fort Simpson, just before leaving that town. The Corporal had the most beautiful little Northwest Territories' puppy we had ever seen, half husky and half malemute, and the O'Learys were the family who had bred him. Sure enough in their yard the parent dogs were staked out. All the puppies were long gone, but had there been another one I would have made a big fuss to buy one. Over the teacups we talked of many things—the new town, the Mackenzie, Canada, the States, Ireland (where the O'Learys were soon to go on their holiday Outside), the world. Teaching school in the town of Wrigley came in for its share too. Along one wall of the living room Mr. O'Leary displayed an imposing collection of slingshots. When questioned about them he said it represented only the spring semester's confiscation from his students: fall would swell the collection even further. He said he had no objection to boys using slingshots except when they were used in his classroom or schoolyard. Each Christmas the weapons were wrapped as gifts and returned to the children along with other gifts at a Christmas party.

We had heard, from Emile Gautreau, that the Indian women of Wrigley were fine craftsmen and that here we might be able to buy moccasins or Crow boots at reasonable prices. Mrs. O'Leary was the mentor of the cooperative venture which insured the women a good market and fair prices. She also kept them inspired enough to work steadily. Unfortunately for us, one of the boats which had passed us was filled with a shipment of moccasins heading for Outside, about five hundred dollars' worth, and not a pair was to be found in the village. Oh well, we would just have to wait 'til Fort Norman.

In about an hour we were on our way again. As we launched the boats, a white man came running down through the crowd of Indians who had gathered to watch us. He was waving a handful of letters. With a gracious apology the Hudson's Bay Factor gave us our mail: it had been mixed in with his own. What a lift to hear from home!

The weather was the most perfect we had experienced, the river calm and very swift. We abandoned our paddling and rafted the kayaks together for a long drift, sprawling about the boats with our legs and arms dangling every which way, reading our mail, chatting, sleeping. We had a dinner of canned foods on a pretty little beach, then rafted together for two and a half more hours. Devon kept his guitar out after dinner and played and sang. There is a song (composed by Antonio Carlos Jobim, recorded by Stan Getz and Joao Gilberto and sung by Astrud Gilberto on a *Verve* label) which, somewhat paraphrased, says, "Quiet nights . . . and quiet chords from my guitar, floating on the silence that surrounds us. Quiet thoughts and quiet dreams, quiet songs on quiet streams . . . oh how lovely." Gene Lees, the translator of the Portuguese lyric, has never floated down the Mackenzie in the summer twilight, but he might well have for the words and music were designed for this.

That night we camped only 110 miles from Fort Norman. The next day a brisk north wind was against us so we made only 23 or 24 miles even though it died in the afternoon and we rafted together and drifted for over two hours. We made camp at a bend of the river and watched a storm march inexorably down on us. It hit just as we were entering the tent for dinner and was over by the time we had finished eating. We immediately went outside to watch the clouds move and to enjoy the clean, washed air. Our camp was in the midst of blossoming wild clover and wild roses in full bloom. The first notice that the storm had passed was given by birds calling, the strange but familiar sound of finches. (Back home the finch has a call of three descending notes, sad and poignant and beautiful, a call which seems to say "Oh dear me." In Canada the last note extends to three triplets, and the call had a different quality to it. We asked Emile Gautreau when we last saw him and he told us that, actually, it *was* a finch we had heard but that his message was "Oh dear Canada, Canada, Canada." Now, back home, I listen for the triplet, and it is not there, and I am a little discontented with my old bird friend.)

The bees returned to the clover and roses and other wild flowers, and the air was filled with their humming. Nick noticed a particularly ugly insect creeping toward him, up the beach from the water, and asked Dev what it was. Dev at once recognized it as a dragonfly nymph and reported that it was about to metamorphose, so we placed a stick in the ground before it and the insect crawled up on it and obligingly proceeded to metamorphose. It actually split down the middle and sort of backed out of its old body in such a fashion that to my uninitiated eyes I had trouble telling which was the old uninhabited insect (so to speak) and which the new. When the process was complete the dragonfly had to dry its wings. Then it flew away, a brilliant success.

On the next day we had another easy drifting day, for over 25 miles, but then the wind changed, coming at us again from the north, and new storms threatened. The river traffic this day brought three huge barge-and-tug combinations going upstream and one motorboat going down. Again that evening we were aware of the dragonflies, but this time in a new rôle: they thrive on mosquitoes. Safely seated behind the tent screen we watched these insect pursuit planes clean the air of marauding mosquitoes, catching them in their legs and crunching them with their strong jaws. We learned when we returned home that in my father's childhood they had been called "mosquito hawks." The dragonflies, by the way, were huge, easily twice as big as any I had ever seen back home.

The next day, Saturday, July 16th, surpassed all previous ones in its calm and beauty. Once more we made a supper stop on a sandbank, then drifted and paddled until 11:30 p.m. We brought a bare minimum of equipment to the tent, and soon rolled into our sleeping bags, but I did build up a nice campfire to undress by, and brewed a pot of coffee while I was at it. We had reason later to be thankful for this fire.

In our sleeping arrangements Devon pitched his private tent a distance in back of ours and slept alone. He had his books and his guitar and usually played a nightly concert before sleeping, a treat we came to regard as our own personal lullaby although he played very softly and, really, only for himself. The younger boys took the inner spots in the tent, then Nick, then my sleeping bag by the roof-to-flooring screen door. Now I know that the man of the house is supposed to sleep across the threshold, as it were, and with his rifle near at hand, to protect the family from all bodily harm, and Nick even did take the outside spot the first night. But I am almost always the last asleep, the first awake, and the lightest sleeper in the family, so we traded places. There is nothing quite like enjoying insomnia when you have the changing scene of the mighty Mackenzie flowing by your door-window. You slip in and out of sleep so that it is never really insomnia at all. We always pitched our tent with several things in mind besides a level site—wind direction, for one thing, and Mommy's View for another. We also made a practice of having the kayaks somewhere in my line of sight in case of sudden wind or oversized wake from passing tugboats.

On this particular night at about 2:00 a.m. I woke up all of a sudden, from no sound that I know of, glanced out of the tent door, and saw a bear in camp. Quickly I reached out and tapped my husband. He sat up quietly, somehow sensing the emergency. I guess it might have been because I had never awakened him before, but Nick was absolutely silent although he had been in deep sleep. I whispered "A bear" and gestured with my head. Nick replied, "The rifle is in my boat!"

Every tale I've ever heard about mean bears raced through my mind, and I've heard dozens of them. But this creature was not a grizzly and there are many more tales which say that the brown bear is more afraid of you than you are of him. I am willing to debate that point but this bear was not. As we sat and stared at him he started shuffling toward us. But the dying embers of the campfire were in his way. A little breeze stirred a whiff of smoke in his direction. He stopped as though shot, looked up, saw the tent, whuffed "Omigosh what am I doing here!", wheeled around and raced up the bank. It was a steep bushy bank but he made it as if teleported and did not rustle even a leaf. Immediately Nick piled out and got the rifle. Then I was brave enough to get out of my sleeping bag and follow him to where we had seen our visitor. The footprints proved we were not dreaming. Back to bed, to sleep, this time with me still next to the door but with the rifle next to me as it was to remain every night for the rest of the trip.

We were truly in bear country, for the next day we passed a huge, beautiful black bear as we drifted. This animal was on the bank as we floated by and took his time about hiding from us. We were now in very scenic surroundings, and for many hours there was not a cloud in sight—most unusual for this part of Canada. As Fort Norman came into view the weather was warm, almost hot, and we were entertaining ourselves with conversation about a cold soda pop at "the Bay." Even though it was a Sunday we figured that the Factor would probably sell us some supplies, Canadian hospitality being what it is. We were unsure of staying overnight. It would all depend. There were three different people who might offer us a campsite, or we could stay on the beach. Still it was an "iffy" thing. And wouldn't a cold soda pop taste good?

At 1:30 that afternoon we reached the Fort, not even having bothered with lunch. Just before landing at the floating dock we passed a spot where three people, two young men and a woman, were sitting on the shore near a motorboat. They weren't exactly working but I decided that they were probably thinking about launching the boat. As we passed by they looked in our direction but called out no greetings.

"Oh well," I thought, "they probably have lots of families in kayaks paddling by their front yards regularly these summers," so I called out a bright "Good Afternoon!"

This brought exactly nothing except "Good Afternoon" right back at me and again I thought, "I wonder if they're trying to get away for a picnic and they're afraid we might detain them. I wonder if. . . ." But no, the men looked much too young for either of them to be the Hudson's Bay manager. By the time we had tied our boats they had roared out into the river. Too late to find out now!

We trudged up a long steep gravel road to the town on top of the bank and into civilization again, but this time there was no one to greet us. It looked as if the whole town had taken advantage of this glorious Sunday afternoon and had swarmed into boats and out on picnics. We knew, though, that the Royal Canadian Mounted Police would be loyally on duty, so we walked a long quarter-mile to his compound. There we checked in with a young man who was in the midst of packing for his new duty station. His replacement was due today, and he would be off to his new assignment in the Yukon tomorrow. He was so busy packing and so excited over the transfer that the presence of five wayfarers from California didn't even bring forth the regular "What brought you to the Mackenzie" comment that we had begun to recognize as our stepping stone to interesting conversation and, indeed, almost as our due. We left him our itinerary, and he recorded it for the new man to pass along to the next station. He also said that the Hudson's Bay man would be quite willing to open the store for us, and that he no doubt had our mail.

Back to the Bay we went only to find the store locked, and no one home at the Factor's house. A man came by on the way to the beach and told us that the Factor and his wife were off on a picnic with a third person. In fact, we had "good afternooned" them at the beach. The next boat taking off, he told us, was being driven by Father Labat, the local priest. This was the third party for whom we would surely have made at least an afternoon stay.

We sat there on the bank looking out over the river, the idle town at our backs, feeling alone and thirsty. There is no store but Hudson's Bay here, and no hotel or restaurant. You can't even find a place to get a drink of water unless you accost some stranger and ask for a handout. As we sat we discussed our situation and tried to make some plans. We would have been delighted to camp in the R.C.M.P.'s yard, or the church's yard, or the Bay's. But the latter two were out of town and the former had not offered, so we were stymied there. The beach was impossible from several standpoints, not the least of which were water supply and sanitation. It was only about 2:30 in the afternoon. We could go for awhile and then make camp.

In the refinery at Norman Wells the one fractionating column produces all the petroleum products needed for the economy of the Mackenzie. The surplus product is the final asphalt, because there are not enough roads in the territory to use all of it.

When the current is so strong that a tug cannot push a heavy string of barges upriver, they are lined along the shore and taken through in stages to gentler waters. Here equipment for an oil exploration venture is being rearranged for such a move. They are tied by thick steel cables to trees well up the bank and ride unmolested until the tug can get around to them.

On the left Nick takes his ease in his drifting kayak. Here on Mills Lake the water is so shallow that only a few minutes of wind builds up white caps. The clouds in this picture are not the kind that come with wind storms.

Norman Wells was only fifty miles, two days' paddle. How was our food supply?

Here we were not in such good shape. We had counted on Hudson's Bay to pad out our last two remaining meals. Four weeks' supply of food awaited us in Norman Wells but we had to get there first. After considering odds and angles we made our decision: we would have our last full dinner tonight, and catch fish and "make do" with leftovers tomorrow. Tuesday we would dine in style at Norman Wells.

We thought we were pretty smart, but we sure pulled a dumb one this time. You'd think with all the weather we had run into we would have been a little less sure of the situation and a little more willing to spend some time sitting there on the bank waiting for people to come home. But the sky was so clear, the weather so perfect, and we were so thirsty. And nobody cared that we were there. We walked down to the dock and climbed into our boats. Just before we left the man who had told us Father Labat was gone said he would be down at Norman Wells on Wednesday and would bring our mail or send it with the Bay man. Thanking him, we shoved off.

By Fort Norman the once-clear Mackenzie and the muddy Liard have finally mingled, and from here on the river is murky. Just below town, however, the Great Bear River enters from the east, and for perhaps two miles there is a thin ribbon of crystal clear blue water along the east shore. We camped along this shore about a mile from town.

Soon after settling in, we saw a speedboat carrying a white man and two Indian youths passing by. We waved. The driver looked carefully at us, then made a wide circle and came in to shore. It was Father Labat, on his way back to Fort Norman. He sat on the bow of his boat and visited with us for over an hour. Father Labat is an Oblate priest and has spent many years in the Far North, ministering to Eskimo and Indian as well as white, and knows this country only as one who has lived in it can. We last saw him on our way home in the airport at Fort Smith. He had been transferred at summer's end to a new pastorate there.

After our visitors had left, Devon and Nick set about to do some serious fishing and in a very short time had pulled in fifteen luscious grayling. We felt much better after dinner, well rested and eager to be on our way. Father Labat had given us some exciting news. Our friend, Duc Meyer, was on the river and four days out of Fort Providence. We turned in early that night, trying to guess where he might be on the river and speculating as to when he would overtake us.

The next day at the start of our traveling the weather was extremely warm. We made good time and had hopes of covering around 35 miles, thereby leaving only 15 miles for the next day's run into Norman Wells, but little by little the character of the weather changed. A cloud cover blocked out the sky and no birds flew along shore. The jaegers whose antics had entertained us for many miles were nowhere in sight. No bird calls came from the trees, but once in awhile a seagull would fly past, squawking dismally, and keeping low to the water. The air felt heavy and oppressive.

The water again took on a glassy appearance and I felt a chill of fear as I remembered the squall which had trapped us near Browning's Farm.

"Let's start looking for a place to hide," Nick called. He must have read my thoughts.

We were right near a place called Prohibition Creek and soon found a likely spot. Even though we hurried, there was barely time to bake a batch of corn bread and heat up soup, chocolate, and coffee. The fish would have to wait for breakfast.

Safe inside we watched what we thought was just another squall move in on us. The wind built up to full gale force. The waves whipped up foaming tops and started pounding the shore in regular combers. Soon our boats were in danger of washing away, so we put on our parkas and rescued them, carrying them a good 15 feet away from the shore. After a bit the wind stopped and, thinking we were between squalls, we all went outside to build a fire and warm up because the temperature had dropped about thirty degrees. A cucumber came riding in on a wave and in great good humor we sliced it and ate it, discussing which tugboat had tossed it over the side. We noticed another shower coming so we retired, still thinking it was just a second squall. But instead it was a windstorm, a real norther, that went on and on and on. Around 1:00 a.m.

I went outside the tent to see how things were doing. No rain was falling, but the wind howled with gusts that almost knocked me over. The water had risen ten feet—not vertically, of course, but along the sloping shore toward our camp. Devon's tent, which he had placed about six feet closer to shore than ours, looked to be in danger of flooding, so I woke him up and he brought his sleeping bag over to ours. For the rest of things, all was well. Our big tent was tied down, the shock cords absorbing the stress of the gusting air with very little evidence of strain.

Inside the tent, though, things were different. The canvas hummed and snapped, the shock cords whined, and the billowing movement of the tent fabric made it seem like the tent was due to cave in at any moment. However, after my checking-up tour, and with Devon in his sleeping bag on one side of me and Nick in his sleeping bag on the other side, I was finally able to stop my useless vigil and fall asleep.

We all slept until 11:00 and awoke to find a steady rain coming down and the wind still at it. By noon we understood that there would be no travel this day, so we started brunch. Nick and Devon stretched a tarp to protect the kitchen and we had what was to be our last filling meal.

Although the overcast remained all day and the wind continued to blow steadily, we had fun. The younger boys alternated between constructing a dam in the creek and coming down to the big beach fire to dry out. We shot the twenty-two at improvised targets. We read, and slept, and played cards, and even went for a walk. Linc found a jug of home-brew which we poured on the campfire to see if it would flare—it did. By suppertime the wind was dying and a promise of lighter sky was in the north, but the meal itself was mighty skimpy.

Then as we sat on logs by the fire and pretended we were full we heard a noise which had been missing during the storm: the sound of an approaching motorboat. Soon we could see it coming from the direction of Norman Wells, keeping no farther than fifty feet off shore and following the contour of the land. It was a Yukon scow, long and narrow, completely open to the elements. The passengers were two young boys and a man. They saw us, waved, and came in to our beach. Before they landed I had the coffee pot on and the fire going.

The boys, Randy and Jimmy, were on their way from their home in Norman Wells to visit for a few days at Fort Norman. At once they joined Brian and Linc in the dam construction project. The man was Mr. Dan Priest, a Pentacostal Missionary whose territory seems to extend from Fort Norman to Fort Good Hope but whose home base is 'at Fort Norman. After two pots of coffee for the adults and mugs of hot chocolate for the boys, it was time for our visitors to be leaving. Just before their departure, Devon, who had broken a guitar string the previous day, asked the younger boys if there were any place in Norman Wells to get a string. The boys said they had a friend there with a guitar like his and maybe he had one—Billy Campbell by name. With this transmission of vital information they climbed aboard their scow. As they pushed off, Mr. Priest handed us a package "to tide us over." We waved our farewells, and as they went around the point we opened the package. Inside were two moose sandwiches. It was the only moose we saw on the entire trip!

Before going to bed we scanned the sky and could see glimpses of blue overhead. The wind was more reasonable now. Feeling very confident about the morrow, I pulled my warm covers over my head and was asleep in minutes, beating the whole family for a change.

I was awakened at half-past two in the morning by Nick shaking me. " 'Nother bear?" I asked sleepily, and reached for the gun.

"No," he said. "I've been lying here worrying for an hour. I think there's another storm coming."

I climbed reluctantly out of my warm, comfortable bed, stepped outside the tent, and looked downstream. Although the sky overhead was relatively clear, sure enough in the distance was the dark warning line that meant storm.

"I think you're right. We'd better get going."

"Shall we eat first?" he asked.

"No. Let's ride for now and see about breakfast later."

"Agreed!" said Nick. "Let's scramble."

We let the little boys sleep, but roused Devon and soon had everything packed except the tent, and the boys' sleeping bags. By three we were on the river, Brian and Linc curled up in the bow of their boats still asleep, and the adults bending a mean paddle to move while we could.

It was gorgeous! For three hours the river stayed calm, the current a good three miles per hour. Our first sign of Norman Wells was the black smoke that rises from the oil refinery's waste-burning stack. After two hours we could see glimpses of the tank farm gleaming in the distance as the sunlight glanced off the silvery metal. But we had a total of 22 miles to go, and our good luck started to wane. Over our left shoulders we could see a squall line moving toward us. What should we do? Try to outrun it? Or head for shore?

There didn't seem to be much choice. We ran for shore, put up the big tent, made a fire, and waited it out. Ironically the squall just edged us. We could have kept going, sneaking along close to the shore, and made two or three miles with only a little dampness. We took down the tent, started to roll it, and then made another error in judgment. The bottom of the tent was muddy from our previous campsite. Now why in the world it hadn't bothered us to roll the tent that way at half-past two in the morning and why we simply felt we had to get that mud off right now at six in the morning, I'll never know. Chalk it up to charming inconsistencies. At any rate, the task, which looked like a five- or ten-minute job, turned out to be a 45-minute job for the mud was extremely gluey and gooey. For the last half hour of our sponging and wiping, the wind was sneakishly making. When we got back on the river it was seven o'clock, we figured we had about seven more miles to go, and we were facing a nasty headwind. For three hours we battled, earning every inch of progress by sheer muscle power. We could see the town clearly now, but it never seemed to get any closer. To our right were huge radio towers. We wondered if they were at the town airport. Then, as we crawled along, we could see telephone poles and wires sticking up from the bush and reasoned there must be a road by them. Still the town remained forever in the distance, the wind grew stronger, and we grew weaker.

At last the moment came when we decided we just could go no farther. We drove for the shore, hauled up the boats, and held a family conference.

"Let's walk it, and come back later for the boats when the wind dies down," said Nick.

"How ignominious!" I thought to myself. "I'm with you," I said aloud.

Up the beach we hiked, in very cheerful spirits. After a few hundred yards we came to a break in the underbrush where a road had been dozered through. We turned onto it and soon were on a broad graveled road, heading for town.

"Food," we exclaimed. "Starving! Starving! Starving!"

"What shall we have for breakfast?" Nick asked.

"Lunch!" said Devon.

"Steak," hollered Linc and Brian.

"Food around the corner," we sang.

From behind us we heard a noise, the old familiar back-home sound of a car. We moved over to the edge of the road and waited. A pickup truck came barreling up with two men in the cab. The driver leaned out the window and greeted us.

"You must be the people Angus Sherwood is expecting. Hop in and I'll drive you to town."

10 «
PARTY TIME

Seated in the back of the pickup truck I was startled at first by the sensation of speed. Devon, noticing my uneasiness, quipped, "Mighty fast current, eh Mom?" The younger boys laughed loudly, "I wonder if there are any rapids." Nick just sat and grinned. Even though we were so hungry our stomachs hurt, we were awash in feelings of triumph. Half our long vacation was over, and here we were without mishap!

In a few minutes our driver, Trevor Morgan, turned into a court and parked with the front bumper up against what looked like a raised sidewalk, which we were soon to find out was a utilidor. Standing on the board sidewalk before a comfortable looking house was Angus Sherwood, a man we had heard of three years and three thousand miles ago, and who, Trevor said, was expecting us. We followed Mr. Sherwood indoors where we were introduced to Mrs. Sherwood and invited to make ourselves comfortable in the living room.

I remember sitting gingerly on an attractive overstuffed chair altogether aware of my filthy stained jeans, my windblown hair, my grubby hands. The boys looked like they hadn't had a bath in three weeks, which was true, and Nick and Dev were right in there too. It seems that standards of personal cleanliness vary in time and place based on a kind of relativity of their own. For example, you might make such children's classifications as "Going to Church clean," "Just home from School clean," and "Two weeks at Y Camp clean." Or for adults, "Dinner at Eight clean," "Let's Barbecue Outside clean," and "Week-end Fishing Trip clean." We couldn't even qualify for "After Burning All the Trash clean" but were in a gamy condition accentuated by being indoors. But I need never have worried. I learned later that the Sherwoods were no strangers to life in the bush. When we walked in, bringing the ingrained smell of campfire and bush dirt, we brought also the key which unlocked a trove of pleasant memories. Far from being offended the Sherwoods were genuinely pleased to see us. They went about putting us at our ease.

Mrs. Sherwood had to prepare her husband's lunch, so she made extra coffee for us. As it was brewing she brought the young boys some soft drinks. Both Brian and Lincoln were doing a remarkable job of concealing their hunger, but Mrs. Sherwood was not a grandmother for nothing. "How about a sandwich?" she said to them.

Both boys nodded eagerly.

"Peanut butter?"

"Oh yes, please," said Brian.

"Ham?"

"Yes, thank you," said Linc.

"You'll want to wash your hands," she smiled, and the boys followed her to the bathroom, uncomplaining for a change. Exclamations of surprise came from the other room. Mrs. Sherwood returned, laughing.

"I guess they didn't expect to see inside plumbing," she said. "We're on the utilidor here."

"Remember, Nick?" I said. "We read about utilidors back home."

"Is that one out in front?" Nick asked. Mr. Sherwood took over: "Yes. It's our heat and water and sewage system. The pipes can't be buried in the permafrost up here, so the engineers put them above ground, then completely cover them over and insulate them. Like above-ground tunnels, they go all over town. These at the Wells are small and wood covered, but wait 'til you see the utilidors at Inuvik. These look very primitive by comparison."

I looked at my dirty hands, then at my new friend. Nick and Dev were looking too. "May we — " I started to ask.

"Of course, people. Make yourselves at home." A little pause. "Perhaps you'd like a sandwich too? We have lettuce and tomato. Cheese. Jam. Ham. Peanut butter."

But I was hung up on those lovely words, "Lettuce and tomato." It had been a month since we had last seen fresh vegetables. Often of late I had found myself daydreaming about crisp hunks of crunchy lettuce. . . .

An hour later we were all acting more like ourselves, feeling comfortable about our full stomachs, and enjoying the wonderful game of getting acquainted with someone new.

Beth and Angus Sherwood have spent all 48 years of their married life in the Northwest Territories. Angus has hunted, fished, traded, owned a sawmill, worked for the government, worked independently, lived in the bush and off the land, lived among Indians, lived in the towns. He is internationally respected as one of the foremost living authorities on the Indians of the Yukon and the Northwest Territories. Beth, a trained nurse, has shared this rugged, adventurous life. They raised and educated their children and watched them move away Outside to follow their own ambitions, then they chose to live their retirement near the Arctic Circle. They never lack friends or interests or things to do. Angus still helps at the Post Office although no longer the Postmaster, having passed the compulsory retirement age. He also manages the Territorial Liquor Store. Through the kindness of our mutual friend, Duc Meyer, we were privileged to meet the Sherwoods, who made our three-day stay at Norman Wells memorable.

After awhile Nick asked about a place to camp along the beach. Since we had not paddled to town we did not know what the shoreline offered. Angus' reply still sticks in my mind.

"Well, I think we can do a little better for you than that," he said.

He led us to a small building across the court from his own dwelling and soon we found ourselves exclaiming over a regular apartment: living room, bedroom, kitchen, laundry and bath. It was on the utilidor system which meant electricity, gas, hot water, and inside plumbing. Even though it would be two or three hours before the wind lapsed into its afternoon lull, thus allowing us to retrieve our kayaks, I could already feel those nice clean clothes we had saved for Norman Wells.

And we would sleep tonight! In the living room was a large couch for Devon. Two sets of box springs from the bedroom were brought out for the boys. Nick and I would use the two mattresses in the bedroom. There were even mirrors, which we really didn't want to look at quite yet, and a refrigerator, with loads of ice cubes. Luxury! This was the schoolmaster's apartment, adjacent to the school and empty for the summer. From time to time it was made available to special transients. We were honored to be so special.

As we stood talking with Angus a car turned into the courtyard.

"Ah" said our host. "That would be John Newton. He is the Superintendent of the Imperial Oil Company Refinery at the other end of town. He has probably come to see if you would like a tour of the plant."

Would we ever!

And the idea that the Superintendent himself was coming to get us was not lost on us either. Dithering just a little, I looked curiously at the tall man in the steel hat who was getting out of the automobile.

"By the way," said Angus, smiling in a way that we were later to recognize as indicating he was enjoying a special joke, "John has already met you."

"Huh?" Nick and Dev and I exclaimed together.

"Yes. In the lobby of the Macdonald Hotel in Edmonton."

"Ohmigosh!" we groaned, and laughed, simultaneously. Mr. Newton, meanwhile, had disappeared across the way into Mr. Sherwood's house.

Angus was really enjoying himself now. "Yes. John was in Edmonton just a month ago. He told me when he got home, 'Angus, I think I've seen your people . . .'" Angus left it at that, chuckling happily. He never did tell us what else Mr. Newton had said, and I couldn't figure how to get him to say more without asking directly, a line of questioning which can only be construed as an exercise in personal vanity. Besides, I wasn't really sure I wanted to know what Mr. Newton had thought of us. I hoped we'd been behaving ourselves, but had we? Were we crabbing at the boys or at each other? Were we overly ostentatious or downright country cousin?

We'll never know, for at that moment John Newton emerged from the Sherwoods' house as we walked across the board sidewalk to meet him.

I still remember his quiet, cordial smile.

"I hear we've met, somewhat." Nick said.

"Yes," replied Newton. "I thought of introducing myself, but then decided to save it. Welcome to Norman Wells!"

Thus began a wonderful afternoon and a new friendship. We toured the town, from one end (that controlled by the government Department of Transport, known as D.O.T.) to the other (controlled by Imperial Oil Company of Canada, Limited, or I.O.L.). We heard more about the problems of heat, light, sanitation, and power, and of the utilidor system which has been developed to solve them. We saw the oil fields where oil comes from underground under such natural pressure that no pumping is needed. A mere capped pipe sticks up out of the permafrost to indicate a well. We walked through the plant where one fractionating column and one control panel supplies all the oil products used up and down the entire 1100-mile Mackenzie, a year-round operation perfectly geared to the economy of the great river, handled in the summer by a crew of about sixty and in the winter by fifteen men less. We saw the steam plant which supplies all the heating for the town, where four ancient railroad engine boilers and one brand new modern boiler roared incessantly, day and night, the raw crude oil being sprayed into them direct from the field, and burning with flames and noise so fierce we could hardly hear even a shout six inches from an ear. I was scared stiff! We stood in the refinery itself, gawking at an operation which must be seen to be believed: it dates back to 1931. Think of a Ronald Searle drawing. Despite its appearance it is a model of simplicity and efficiency.

The guided tour ended and now Mr. Newton extended another invitation: a cocktail party, at his home, at 8:00, to meet a few people. Bring the young boys too. He had boys of his own, about the same age, and there would be lots for them to do. Of course we accepted. Mr. Newton then drove us across town again, dropped Brian and Linc at the Sherwoods' and then drove Nick and Dev and me out to the spot along the road between two and three miles south of town, to where we estimated we were opposite our beached boats. With promises to be ready at 8:00 when he would pick up the Sherwoods and us at home, we waved goodbye and plunged into the bush to find our way to the riverside and our kayaks.

Rollicking along at the edge of the current we arrived at the beach called the "mud dock" in half an hour. A few more minutes and we had carried our sleeping bags and stuffbags up the fifty-foot embankment to our new home and were queued up for showers. Here we discovered a peculiarity of the older utilidors. If you live close to the end of the service area the cold water pipes grow warm from the nearby hot water pipes so that you are supplied with two temperatures of water: very warm and much too hot. By using the cold water tap we all took nice hot showers of perfect temperature. By using the ice in the refrigerator we took care of our thirst with nice cold water. We also took care of another thirst by buying a carton of beer and stocking the refrigerator for future use.

In the bottom of each stuffbag was a cache of clean clothes. I had a neat white blouse and the capris and sweater I had worn on the plane to Edmonton, the others had clean jeans and new turtleneck shirts. Nick trimmed his month-old beard to a Sheriff-of-Nottingham style, while Dev shaped his to a Telegraph Avenue Special. Linc and Brian, who had needed haircuts a month before vacation even started, combed their shaggy locks in the latest rock and roll fashion. I had been wearing my hair in a long braid but tonight I coiled and netted it in a pug. Washed and combed and dressed so fine, we said temporary farewells to the Sherwoods and started walking to the restaurant for dinner.

Norman Wells is a most unusual town. As I mentioned before, it is divided into two parts, one-half owned by the government (DOT) and one-half by private industry (IOL). Some services are shared in common, such as the light and heat and water and sewage service supplied through the utilidor pipes. Other services are "separate but equal," in a sense, as in the case of the graded schools. Each part of town has its own store, in the one a company store, in the other a government store. DOT personnel may not shop at the IOL store, and vice versa. (Interestingly enough the tourist may not shop at DOT or IOL either, a fact which is neither concealed nor revealed in the travel guides of the region.) The recreation hall is in IOL territory, but membership and facilities are open to the whole town. The same goes for the curling rink and the softball park. The church building, too, is located on the IOL side but it is meant for all. It houses both Roman Catholic and Protestant denominations, being divided neatly in two by a wall partition. The Post Office is IOL but the airport and terminal is DOT. The Territorial Liquor Store is DOT. Both DOT and IOL have their own mess halls for their own employees, but neither is open to the public. For meals the tourist must go to the Mackenzie Mountain Hotel, on DOT land, a mile and a half from town at the crossroads of the road to the airport and the road to the radio transmitters. It was the latter we had seen that morning and wondered if they were airport towers. The town itself is between one and two miles long. Now we were heading for dinner at the hotel.

But before we could get there we had one more errand to do. While the two men and I were paddling the boats the two younger boys had made a friend. This boy and his little sister were reading comic books in the front room of our apartment when we came home. Apparently big deals had been made to arrange some book trading. We asked the boys to introduce their friend but, names being of no importance, they had to turn to him to introduce himself.

"My name is Billy Campbell."

"Hup" said Dev, "The Bill Cambell who plays the guitar?"

So we had to pause at Billy's to buy a string, and finally we were on our way. A mile and a half seems like a good-sized walk, but again we were rescued by Trevor and his pickup truck. Soon we stood outside the unmarked Mackenzie Mountain Hotel, and, rather hesitantly, followed Trevor's directions and headed for the wooden steps he said led to the dining room.

The hotel looked like none you ever see in the United States. A cluster of three or four large aluminum trailers, somehow interconnected, formed the establishment. We walked down a board floor hall, turned right through a screen door, and found ourselves in a little room with three white painted tables at one end and a kitchen at the other. Low, wooden, backless benches formed the seats. A taciturn cook regarded us from behind the counter.

"Good evening," Nick smiled. "We are the party Mr. Sherwood phoned about."

"Roast-beef-tonight-you-all-want-soup?" our man spoke.

We all said "you bet" and sat down. Out came the cook, now the waiter, with a huge bowl of homemade vegetable soup, a handful of small bowls, and a ladle.

"Help-yourselves-it's-hot," he said, and walked away.

No second invitation was needed. Crackers were on the table, along with spoons, knives and forks thrust into water tumblers.

When our man returned we had cleaned the big bowl and were raving about the soup. We saw him almost smile. Down on the table he plunked five warmed plates, a huge platter of. sliced beef, a great mound of whipped potatoes, a bowl of gravy, a green vegetable, and two salads — one fruit and one tossed green. We cleaned all the plates and were starting in on the bread and butter when he appeared with a fresh berry pie. It was gorgeous. The crust was superb, the filling excellent. We were lavish in our praise, and the empty plates testified to our sincerity.

By coffee time our taciturn cook was now our genial cook. He poured himself a cup of coffee, lit a cigarette, and joined us.

"I hear you people have had quite a trip on our river," he began.

This was our first meeting with Big Al Wilson, a man we came to like and respect, and whose cooking we greatly enjoyed.

Seated at the table sipping coffee and listening to the men
I found myself thinking of our cold and hunger and worry of
the night before. I remembered Thoreau's words concerning
our cluttered lives, "Simplify, simplify. Instead of three meals
a day, if it be necessary eat but one; instead of a hundred
dishes, five; and reduce other things in proportion." I thought
how much easier to follow his philosophy when the element of
choice was present. Yesterday, when out of supplies, we had
no choice and the forced simplification seemed like great hard-
ship. Today we looked forward to one real meal per day but
because it was our choice the task was easy. Each meal at the
hotel cost $3.00. Three times five people times breakfast, lunch,
and dinner equals $45 times three days equals $135 which is
ridiculous. So we figured to make do on hot chocolate in the
morning, a snack at the Rec in the afternoon, and one of Big
Al's monumental dinners in the evening. Thoreau had the right
idea.

Finally we had to leave, with promises to return the next
day. We walked back to the Sherwoods' house in plenty of
time for our date.

While riding to the Superintendent's house in his car John
Newton told us, "I knew you would be tired after four weeks
on the river. I figured you'd be so tired you wouldn't care to
meet anybody, or so tired you wouldn't care if you met everybody — so I invited everybody!"

First we met Mrs. Marjorie Newton, a woman of charm
and intelligence, an excellent hostess who soon made us
welcome.

And then the guests started to arrive. As John had said, we
met "everybody" including the local Roman Catholic priest,
the Protestant minister, the Company doctor, and the Wells
postmaster (a woman, Mrs. Trevor "Cookie" Morgan). All who
were unencumbered or who could possibly get a babysitter
came. I think they even shared the babysitters on shifts, for
young couples kept coming and going all evening. This was a
party, an occasion, and all were dressed accordingly; the men
in coats and ties, the women in summer frocks with right acces-

sories. Yet not an eyebrow was raised, and not a remark even implied about our casual appearance.

Naturally enough at first the conversation centered about Nick and me. Soon a group of women were clustered about Nick and I was holding court for a group of men. Then after the men had been satisfied with my version of why I like camping and the women had asked Nick for his answers to similar questions, the circles changed. The interested women, I discovered, wanted mainly to know at what age do you start bringing children on these kinds of kayak trips, what do you eat, and how do you persuade your husband to take you with him on these trips? The men asked Nick, at what age do you take your children, what do you eat, and how do you persuade your wife to come along?

But as the party warmed up we were less and less like novelties and more and more like people, and soon the old conversational give and take was zinging right along. It seems there are some universal topics for discussion even at Norman Wells. For one thing, families are relatively transient, coming for stays of two to three years. No roots are put down in such a short period and. . . . For another thing, there are many children and limited recreational facilities, therefore. . . . Then the schools are. . . . And the churches. . . . And the men are never home, they work such long hours. . . . And the women coffee and bridge all day. . . . And during the summer there are no jobs for the teenagers. . . .

It sounded just like home.

They also found television a problem, their problem being that they didn't have any. Another topic that was scarcely mentioned was Viet Nam, but Canadian politics were aired here and there although usually in contexts we could not follow. Another subject on which we were totally lost was the sport called "Curling." Apparently it is a way of life in the Mackenzie and the Yukon. For some, curling itself makes the whole winter worth it. By twelve midnight I was ready to stay through 'til spring just to try.

By 1:00 a.m. the party thinned out, and by 2:00 it died. Next day was a working day, and even though the darkness refused to come, a few hours of sleep were necessary for the work of the Wells. But for the first time in our lives we had the incomparable experience of not having to worry about when to leave a really swinging party: we were passengers in the host's car, therefore couldn't leave 'til he took us. (I heartily recommend this setup as a way to have a good time, particularly if protocol on arrivals and departures bewilders you.)

Devon, who had been introduced to two college-age girls, and Brian and Linc, who had played every boy game imaginable with the three younger Newton sons, were finally ready to go home. But I think that John and Marjorie and Nick and I could have kept right on talking until breakfast. As we all said of each other, "It seems like we've known you forever."

We drove home in the bright 2:00 a.m. light and soon were comfortably settled on our real mattresses.

"I think I just might not even get up tomorrow," Nick said as he drifted off to sleep.

"Mm," I answered, meaning "Me too."

But I found myself thinking warmly of new friends and washing machines and all the chores I would do in the morning.

II «
CANOL

On Thursday, July 21st, at 10:30 a.m., I went to a Coffee Hour at the home of Mrs. Trevor Morgan. About twenty women were there, most of them in pretty print frocks, heels and hose. The best china, the long-cherished silver, the nicest linens were used to serve a variety of home-baked delicacies. Such pleasure to drink coffee from a fragile cup instead of a thick navy mug! Many little children played outside in the yard, and one infant and two or three toddlers came indoors with their mothers. It was like the Coffee Hours I had enjoyed long ago as a young wife and mother when we lived in married university student housing, and it was an experience I never in the world expected to have in the Far North.

Before we came to the Mackenzie I did my best to learn something about the country and its people: I looked in the Reader's Guide for books, the Periodicals Guide for articles, and wrote to the Canadian Government Travel Bureau for every pamphlet they could send me. I bought detailed charts of the river, and the most recent river pilot log. We talked with Duc Meyer who had made three river trips of his own, and knew something of what to expect. Still I never imagined I would be sitting in a living room near the philodendron in the corner visiting with such well-groomed, charming, interesting people as the women at Norman Wells.

These women showed, in a very short time, much of the white family's way of life in an isolated but modern town. Because of air transportation, amenities are available that were undreamed of even fifteen years ago. For example, although staples and non-perishables are brought in yearly by tug and barge, and frozen foods are brought on refrigerator barges, perishables such as fresh fruits, vegetables, dairy products, and

meats are delivered weekly by air all year round. The current
movies are regularly shown, free, at their community recreation center. Mail service, again by air, is almost daily. A bush
pilot charter over the nearby mountains to Trout Lake for a day
of fabulous fishing is a summer outing. A couple of days in the
bright lights of Edmonton, just a few hours away by scheduled
airline, is as much routine to them as a San Franciscan's flight
to Seattle or Los Angeles.

I was astonished at the lack of provincialism in this isolated
territory. At no time is the Mackenzie regarded as the "boon-
docks" of Canada by the people who dwell there. They feel that
the world problems are their problems too, and that the future
of the Northwest will be as much determined by what goes on
Outside as by what happens in their own local government.
There is a universality too about some of the ordinary problems
of just being women, wives, and mothers. For one, they particularly wanted to know more about combining marriage,
motherhood and a career. Canada, they said, is at least a generation behind the United States in this respect. How did I do
it? I could only tell them that from my experience you must
have the whole-hearted approval of your family; without that,
forget it.

They also asked me many questions about meal planning for
this particular trip, so we made a date for that afternoon when
Nick and I would be packing the next four weeks' food in our
two waterproof boxes. Most of the women came, and all afternoon Nick and I demonstrated and explained and answered
questions while we worked. The menus came from many years
of experience and many weeks of planning. Our family uses
dried and dehydrated foods packed by the DriLite Company of
Lynwood, California. From their lists I based our dinners
around 15 different main dishes: steak, chicken and noodles,
chili and beans, pork chops, Spanish rice with beef, scalloped
potatoes with ham, beef and vegetable stew, hamburgers, bean
pot, macaroni and chili, corn chowder, beef hash and gravy,
savory potato stew, bean mulligan, and beef Stroganoff. Using
a variety of DriLite items, such as fruit drinks, soups, vegetables, puddings, and baking mixes, these were all packaged as

well-balanced meals. Each complete meal for five was packaged separately in a plastic bag and numbered.

Breakfasts were more standardized, consisting of three egg-type meals alternating with three pancake-type. For example, one morning might be orange juice, ham and scrambled eggs, biscuits, butter, jam, hot chocolate, and coffee; the next morning pineapple-grapefruit juice, bacon, pancakes, maple syrup and butter, chocolate, and coffee. The pancakes were varied by adding bits of dried fruit to the batter, or fresh blueberries when we came upon them or honey or jam for a topping. The eggs were sometimes served plain, or with onion flakes and bits of ham and bacon, or as an omelet. (Yes, the eggs are dried and dehydrated. Yes, they are delicious. No, they are not like anything you ever tasted during World War II or on the last fathers' and sons' overnight.) And often we had the freshest fish in the world.

Biscuits and corn bread and gingerbread and cobblers and cakes I baked in a folding camp oven. Years ago I battled, more or less successfully, with reflector ovens. On the Yukon, Devon designed and built a campfire oven out of No. 10 tins and coat hangers. But this year the sporting goods companies came out with an excellent product and a favorite aunt and cousin sent one to us as a bon-voyage gift. It proved a treasure. From a package with the dimensions of 12 x 12 x 2 inches unfolds an oven of 12 x 12 x 12 inches, with a thermometer in its door face. I had a sturdy grid measuring 14 x 28 inches which gave me room to do my baking over one half the cook fire simultaneously with boiling or broiling over the other half.

Among our cooking gear I also had the following: one griddle, one folding fry-pan, one five-quart pot with lid, one sauce pan with lid. These were Teflon coated. Our coffee pot was a veteran of forty years' camping, and looked it. Knives, forks, spoons, cooking tools, screwdriver, pliers, sharpener, and can opener were kept in a canvas pocketed "tool case" which I sewed together after getting the idea from an item in a Boy Scout camping catalog. We ate from plain aluminum plates and drank out of war surplus mugs — two-cup size, no handles.

Each boat also carried an aluminum cup for use en route so that the cook kit, once packed, would not have to be disturbed.

Lunches were generally simple foods that could be eaten without cooking, such as punch, peanuts, cheese and crackers, dried fruits, and candy. However, I tossed in extra chocolate drink and about three dozen packets of dried soups in case of need, and this proved to be a worthy provision.

All told we had food for 45 days. We knew we could stretch this and we planned on buying meals in towns and supplies at Hudson's Bay stores. As it worked out, our calculations were very good. We had variety, quality, quantity. The women at Norman Wells made a flattering audience while we did our packing, and by mid-afternoon we not only finished our re-packing but had a lot of ego-building fun as well.

For dinner we hitchhiked to Big Al's again where we ate boiled and buttered fresh lake trout. Al said he learned to pre-pare fish this way from the Indians. The process is more like poaching than boiling, and the results are delicious. Once again we ate everything he placed before us. We looked around hopefully for more fresh pie, but not tonight: "You have to be in the mood to bake," he said, demonstrating the true tempera-ment of the master chef. So we finished up with canned man-darin oranges.

This evening we shared our dinner conversation with a heli-copter mechanic, a long-time bush pal of Big Al's. These two men of the North kept up a wild banter of jokes and anecdotes. One of the stories the mechanic told was about when he win-tered one year on the polar ice. He said that the silence can be so profound that when you turn in at night you hear your own heartbeat, unfamiliar head noises, and even what must be the sound of your own blood circulating.

We walked back to the Sherwood's house and spent an hour visiting, when John came to take us to his house for the eve-ning. The superintendent's quarters are near a little creek, somewhat apart from the company compound. The house stands at the edge of the river, overlooking Goose and Bear Islands in mid-stream and the deserted landing area for the Canol Project on the far side. Many of the oil wells are on these islands and company river traffic passes regularly from shore to shore. This house had the only picture windows we saw in the Mackenzie, and they stretched the length of the 30-foot living room. Marjorie said she never tired of watching the daily changes in the river and that the seasonal changes were magnificent. The house had been shipped by barge across from Canol, and redesigned and furnished especially for the IOL superintendent whose duties included many social ones. A stop at Norman Wells, we learned, is a must for all VIP's who travel the Mackenzie. We were not in this category, but enjoyed being treated as though we were. It did not take much imagination to picture some of the interesting gatherings that take place there because of the Wells' unique contribution to that country's economy.

The Newton boys and our younger boys went to the movies while we adults looked at John's 35-millimeter slides and learned more about year-round living in the North. His photography was superb. Cold weather doesn't keep those people inside if the day has no wind and the mood demands a picnic. We saw pictures of freeze-up and break-up, dog sleds and snow cats, championship curling teams and amateur night entertainments. We saw the slides of a laundry which burned down the night of a mid-winter company party in weather so cold that the water froze on its way from the hoses to the fire, therefore the fire had to be "enjoyed" rather than fought. Then we saw a collection of arctic wild flower pictures among which we all recognized fireweed, but the names of very few others were known to John.

When we left we had another date for the next day: a trip to Canol. Just that afternoon on the way to Canol a bulldozer had hopelessly bogged down in the muskeg. John and Trevor planned to go over to get an idea of the recovery problem, and there was room for Nick and me.

We were waiting on the beach at 9:00 a.m. For the first time in five days the late morning air was quiet, the water serene and polished, and the temperature in the high 70's. Soon we were speeding across the river in Trevor's powerful little outboard, to beach a few minutes later on the sand and then walk up the old graveled road to the Canol site. A hundred yards from shore we saw the first abandoned truck, lying wheels up in the brush just as it had apparently landed when it rolled off the side of the road 20 years before. A little later we passed about a 14-foot section of four-inch pipe, all that was left, John said, of the 750 miles of pipeline laid so laboriously over 20 years ago. We continued up the road, passing other derelicts, until we reached the top of the bank where the land leveled off again and an old truck was parked. This truck, long written off as useless, was just barely operable. The connection between the steering wheel and the front wheels was like that between a poorly-rigged tiller and a loose rudder; the truck felt like it was swimming up the chuckholed road. We had almost five miles to navigate, so we held on and hoped.

Not much has been written about the Canol Project. During World War II, when for awhile it looked like Allied oil shipment to Alaska might be cut off, someone decided to run a pipeline from Norman Wells through 750 miles of subarctic muskeg and over a mountain range to White Horse in the Yukon Territory of Canada. CANOL was the army base, U. S. operated and supplied which cared for 4500 men, 3000 on the post and 1500 in the field. The project was completed, costing $400,000,000. One million barrels of oil were pumped, which is mighty expensive oil, even for wartime. When you consider that the annual output of the Wells is in the tens of thousands of barrels you can also see what an impact this had on the oil fields too. Within a year the line was abandoned for a variety of reasons, only one of which was the extremely restrictive diameter of the pipe.

Of greatest interest to us, however, was the fact that there is no way to junk anything in this region. Shipping costs are so high that after the war it was economically unfeasible to peddle the army base as scrap. Dealers came through and skimmed a little cream, a few small buildings were dragged on skids to barges and moved to new locations up and down the river, but for the most part a deserted camp for thousands of men sits and slowly moulders back into the bush.

What a sight to see, this old ghost camp! Rusting army vehicles were scattered everywhere. Old G.I. signs with familiar G.I. directives could still be deciphered at the motor pool and on many buildings. Hundreds of pallets of spare parts marched row on row between long storage buildings. Thousands and thousands of truck items in excellent condition sat in the bins in these buildings — steering wheels, fenders, bumpers, springs, fans, fan belts, engine blocks, crankshafts, pistons, clutches, brakes and gears, all vintage 1942. And they would cost a fortune to move.

We walked through a mess hall which could seat over 1000 men. Huge coffee urns, bright and gleaming, and showing no signs of deterioration, stood near the kitchen area. Trevor and John walked across the still-sound floor and remarked about what a recreation hall this would make if only it could be moved to Norman Wells. We went through the base hospital, through barracks made of interconnected Quonset huts, through the power station which, oddly enough, stored a marvelous amount of large neat cast-iron pot-bellied stoves. (You could sell them tomorrow for mountain cabins, but how to get around the cost of shipping them there?) We went out to the hangars. We looked across the landing strips, all much overgrown and totally useless. We drove out the road toward the Yukon, but in less than half a mile we were stopped by a washout. We walked out a way and looked far up the cleared path to where toiling G.I.s had once hacked out a pipeline. We stopped and admired a set of fresh moose prints made by the only traffic that could now travel this road. Then we got in the truck and started back for the boat. On the way we took a final look at the stuck bulldozer. The IOL men decided it might take two bulldozers rather than one to pull it out, but they would see what one would do first. On our way back down the hill we met the rescue party coming up. By noon we were speeding across the river to town.

As John drove us home we saw what looked like two large freight canoes, under two different sailing rigs, rafted together. At the tiller of one a bare-chested white man was sitting. There

The motor pool at CANOL looking across toward Normal Wells and the Franklin Mountains. The small building at the left was once a checking station for vehicles about to go on the bush road built by the GI's between this site and Whitehorse, Yukon.

Veterans of World War II who served in the Far North will remember the Quonset Hut barracks. Here they stand, still largely weather tight, as abandoned 20 years ago in CANOL.

Devon elects to sail, using a sheet of plastic. The stunted trees on the bank reflect the influence of poor soil and scanty precipitation. Far from being a land of much snowfall, the Northwest Territory is often called "The Arctic Desert."

While Brian busily reads a comic book, the author talks to one of the family by radio. These walkie-talkies proved more fun than practical because of their limited range.

were other people in the boats, and some appeared to be swimming alongside, but we could not see how many.

In about an hour our curiosity was satisfied. They were indeed freight canoes, one with a lateen rig, the other with a Viking-style squaresail. In them were five young men, whom the boys immediately named "The Pirates." Truly, they presented a swashbuckling appearance with their camp-soiled jeans and their sheath knives at the hip. All were strong and bronzed by their rugged river life, and bearded, except for one young man whose whiskers were slow-growing, and they wore their hair very long. Among their helter-skelter gear they carried three guitars. They had an assortment of improvised, well-used equipment that indicated many things to an experienced camper: low budget, for one, and great skill in inventiveness and adaptability, for another. Brian and Lincoln had left to investigate the weather station south of town. Nick and I were feeling very middle-aged — the young men were displaying beautiful manners, including "yes sirs" and "no ma'ams" accompanied by deference due. But Devon, almost 20 years old, was their contemporary and by degrees we eased out of the talking while he took over.

Our Pirates, later called "The Beatles" by the townspeople along the river, were as follows: Paul and Andy Fisher, 21 and 23, brothers from England; George Day, 21, Edmonton, Alberta; Rod Copeland, 23, Montreal, Quebec; and Rob Caldwell, 20, Galt, Ontario.

The two young men from England were working their way around the world. When they came to North America they wanted to see how far north they could get and reached Yellowknife which, they thought, was the end of the line because the road ends there. They came upon the three Canadians who were holding down summer jobs in the mines, and the five of them got acquainted. Somehow they came up with the idea of moving farther north via the river, so they pooled resources, bought canoes, and took off. Their goal was Inuvik where they were confident they would be able to find jobs even though they were repeatedly told that their chances were poor. Devon made a date to see them after dinner, and we left as they were putting up their tent on the shore near the mud dock.

Meanwhile Brian and Linc had found their way to the weather station and watched the fascinating process of sending aloft a balloon and recording exotic data. They returned with such a lilt in their steps that it was impossible to keep from being moved by their excitement. This had been the first "field trip" of their own organization, one not promoted by Mommy or Daddy or school or Scouts or whatever, but all their own. They had been treated with the greatest courtesy. Linc's prize souvenir of the station is a 12-inch strip of recording tape on which one of the technicians had written out the interpretation of all data regarding the particular balloon the boys had watched. The men at the station were: Al Skare (officer in charge), Lyle Bligh, Robert Charles Brown, Bill Prent, and Ken Simpso. The boys will never forget them and that adventuresome afternoon.

Dinner again, and for the last time, was at the Mackenzie Mountain Hotel. Here our younger boys had another fast friend: Harold, Big Al's foster son. We left them playing there on Harold's brand new bike, when we walked back to Sherwoods'. We spent the evening until 10:00 visiting with these wonderful people. They told us of their early life in the North, before plane transportation, when mail came in the summertime only, except for an occasional message brought by dog sled. We heard of some of their business ventures, including the sawmill Angus once owned which had turned out most of the wood for the Canol Project (something like 4,000,000 board feet). Angus also gave me the names of a dozen different books on the North, for winter reading and, perhaps, to inspire a return visit.

We said our goodnights, then walked across to the apartment. Devon, we knew, was somewhere with the Pirates. We wondered if Brian and Linc had come back, for the weather had turned squally. Imagine our pleasure when we heard the sound of music from the little house. Inside were all six young men, Brian and Linc, loads of beer and soda pop, and a hootenany in progress. They were all having such a marvelous time that our entrance did not produce the slightest damping effect.

The singing and guitar playing continued well past midnight. Many were the songs I remembered from Scout camp days, the only place I ever heard folk singing when I was a girl. There were even a couple of songs now labeled "protest" which we used to sing with great girlish enthusiasm, under the label "Revival." The hootenany that night included folk, spiritual, protest, revival, and rock, plus other songs too hard to categorize. It was grand. By the end of the party we were all good friends, with addresses exchanged and plans to meet again in Inuvik. We were all eager to be on the river the next day, although we did not plan to travel together, and so "goodnight."

Saturday morning brought bright weather but a north wind. We looked anxiously at the white-capped water and talked things over as we walked out to Big Al's for breakfast. We decided that the best plan was to wait for the afternoon calm, then leave even if we could only get ten or fifteen miles along our way. As with Odysseus in the Land of the Lotos-Eaters, we were too comfortable at Norman Wells, and too many tempting invitations were making us unmindful of the journey ahead. That same evening a dance was scheduled at the Rec. Sunday a charter was flying to a lake just beyond the mountains for some marvelous fishing. "Why not stay a little longer?" they asked us. We knew we had to leave.

We passed the time walking around taking pictures and watching the river's surface. Not until 4:00 did the wind finally abate, and we trooped to Sherwood's house to say farewell. How easy it was to decide to go, and how difficult to leave! The Newtons had told us to be sure to phone them as we left so that they could take pictures, but a call to their house found John not yet home from work, so it was goodbye by phone.

At last we were at the mud dock, seated in our kayaks, and ready to go. The Pirates too, responding to the same inner urge that counseled us to leave while we could, were breaking camp. We pushed off into the current and headed north, waving and calling back to the young men.

A few hundred yards downstream, we heard a great clamor of auto honking and people shouting from the bank. There on the shore were the Newtons, their children, and another young couple by the name of Shaw. They stopped their cars, piled out on the bank, waved their cameras and called wildly. Naturally we pulled right in, to say our real goodbyes and to restage our departure for the benefit of the clicking cameras.

12 «

SANS SAULT RAPIDS

Two hours and ten miles out of town we pulled over to camp near a little creek. Along the opposite shore of the river a good two miles away we spotted the Pirates' canoes. The wind blew from the south and they were under full sail, fairly flying along at the edge of an approaching storm. They were soon out of sight. Behind us we could still see the smoke from Norman Wells and hear the occasional sound of a plane or helicopter taking off. We had to be a little careful walking around on the beach for there was a high water line of oily rocks and drift-wood from the refinery processes. But even with these remind-ers that civilization was not so very far away, it felt good to be back in the bush again.

After dinner, while rain pelted down, we sat and talked about adventures in town, particularly those of the younger boys. We marveled at how they had been able to find their way around and to get places so quickly. Nothing to it, they told us, you simply walk on the utilidors. If it rained, you just ducked under them until the shower passed. In addition to two evening movies and the weather station, the boys had also taken in two matinees and a church treasure hunt, making friends from one end of town to the other. All three Newton boys were pestering their parents to let them grow their hair long and neither Brian nor Linc helped the situation one bit by admitting that back home they preferred close-cropped haircuts. Instead they pulled out pocket combs and preened. Finally, they told us that the best part of all was, "We hardly ever saw you! We just had fun!" and then a hasty, "No offense, folks."

We went to bed on the hard sandy ground talking about the dance that was going on back in town but not regretting it one bit. Although we had just spent three nights on mattresses, the ground didn't feel so bad after all, and we had a good sound sleep. The next day had us fighting a head wind again, trying to reach Oscar Creek, a place that had been highly recommended for both camping and fishing. We had to hole up along a rocky beach for a little over two hours, with less than three miles left to go. The moment the wind died down we shoved off, but in so doing I ripped a part of the stern keel strip from my boat and we had to pull in again. In reconditioning the boats back home Nick had replaced and glued two bow keel strips and one stern keel strip. The one giving us the trouble was the one he had not replaced. It was idle to deplore.

An hour later we were launched again, and paddling with all our might for Oscar Creek, racing the weather. It proved to be another Camp Dismal, but heavy showers were on us and we had no choice but to stay. The river had recently dropped, leaving a thin shell of dry sand and rock over a thick quagmire. One misstep and you were in mud to your ankles. It took a lot of maneuvering to locate the tent and chart safe paths to the clear creek water. The place had evidently been well used for there was little driftwood for cooking and campfire. But after a very good dinner everyone's spirits picked up and we went fishing. We discovered many fresh tracks in the mud including moose, bear, and large birds, probably cranes.

Though we had high hopes for the next day, leaky boats delayed our departure until 1:30. The water had an ominous glassiness again, but we paddled fiercely for about two hours and found a tiny cove for shelter just barely in time. Great crashes of thunder and sluicing rain came down only seconds after all was secure, but we were old hands now. The family slept away the afternoon while I puttered around under a tarp stretched in front of the tent. Later on, with coffee, juice, beans, and corn bread, and a huge bonfire started between showers we felt great and cribbage after dinner made the evening's entertainment. It didn't really matter that in three days we had come only 25 miles from Norman Wells. We had seen what our tent could do in a storm, and we were dry. We were on a beach so covered with driftwood that there must have been a hundred thousand dollars' gift shoppe inventory to send up in smoke, and we were warm. We had plenty of supplies, and we were fed.

Nothing stirred on the river for the next two days. On the opposite shore from us about two miles distant we made out the shape of a beached motorboat and shelter. Now and then we would look across through our field glasses, but we never saw a person or a sign of campfire. They left the evening of the second day, and we often wondered what they did to pass the time. It looked like they just huddled in the boat with a shelter over their heads. This is not our family's way when the weather turns foul.

Camping even at its best is a lot of hard work. The chores performed so quickly and easily at home are often long and complicated in camp. Carrying water, preparing food, cooking, cleaning up—each has its own particular problem not directly encountered at home. A person forgets that a house is constructed on plumb lines and with level floors and that a camp is not. Things in camp are always slopping and spilling until you recognize the problem and solve it. Out of doors there are lights and shadows not encountered in our modern indirect-lighted homes and businesses. You find yourself squinting in the sunlight or snatching off your sunglasses in the shadows. Seldom is the temperature just right. With no furnace to turn up or turn down you are forced constantly to adjust your clothing. Since the air is rarely perfectly still, no-draft ventilation is merely a slogan, and the breeze can be a curse or blessing depending on the air temperature, the time of day, the activity. Add to this such human foibles as headaches, food idiosyncrasies, and aversion to manual labor and the camping scene starts looking bad. Then substitute surly weather for idyllic sunshine and unless you watch it things can be awful.

There are, of course, ways to get around these inconveniences. The fact that it is nicer to be comfortable than uncomfortable probably explains as well as anything the reason we mire ourselves so deeply in civilization. But if you add to your camping gear a Coleman stove and its fuel supply and to your

kayak a one and a half-horsepower kicker and its fuel supply
you have added a new dimension to your outdoor environment
and have taken your first step away from primitive camping.
From there it is step by step to a trailer or a summer cabin
which, while great fun, are not quite the same thing at all.

However, roughing it need not be an endurance test. I, for
one, find no personal satisfaction in living off the land, testing
my resistance to cold, and showing an obnoxious out-doorsiness
in a dozen other ways. Therefore, on our gypsy trips, we always
have some special items which are usually brought with everyone's knowledge and consent, but sometimes sneaked along.
We include such things as a pocket-sized cribbage board,
checker set, and chess set; a book of riddles; a Shakespeare
and a Bible; a half-dozen racy paperbacks, science fiction and
mystery stories; crossword puzzles; several decks of playing
cards; paper and pencils; comic books; a bird book; musical
instruments; and when possible, a gin bottle.

Clothes are carefully planned for convenience, efficiency,
comfort; changes being kept to an absolute minimum: one set
on, one set drying, one partial set in case of emergency. Safety
and first aid come in for a lot of planning. For one thing, no
matter how bothersome, we always wear our life jackets in the
boats. Sleeping gear and weather protection, including tentage,
is the best we can buy. Food is planned to entice as well as fill.
But it's still a lot of hard work to be successful at any kind of
camping, from knapsack to cabin, and when the weather sours
and you're holed up it takes at least a "starter" to keep the
entire venture from souring too.

I am the "starter" in our family. When the weather zeros
in on us, we all find ourselves totally willing to stay in our
sleeping bags catching up on sleep and wishing the storm away.
But after awhile I get hungry. And a strong cup of black coffee
thinks marvelous. And wouldn't a great big bonfire feel good?

I look at the lazy people I live with, snuggled warm and un-
conscious in their bags, and I can hardly wait to shiver into
heavy clothes and get outside. Wind in hair and rain on face
feel good, fire feels better, hot coffee best yet! It's good to be
up and awake and have the whole scene to myself. After
awhile, though, sympathy for the family takes over and I pre-

pare more coffee and hot chocolate. I serve the lazy ones their brew, for they are awake by now but still not stirring from their sacks. Little by little life returns and they start enjoying the novel experience of being outdoors in such absurd weather.

Never yet have we had a "sour" camp because of bad weather. I sometimes wish that one of the others had the "starter" temperament, but it's too late now to educate them. They can outsleep me by hours. I'm the one with the appetite and the coffee head. The lines are drawn. So be it.

We spent two full days and three nights in our little cove letting the storm continue at its own pleasure, as the ancient Egyptians used to do. Brian involved himself the first day in constructing an elaborate catch-basin and dam, working steadily with the one camp shovel and ordering around anyone who presumed to help him. He found two hollowed pieces of wood to serve as flumes, placed them in the seeps along the bank, directed a stream of water to his artificial lake, then engineered what he hoped would be a spillway. Then he had to wait the night through to allow the lake to fill before he could see if it would work. Alas, during the night the wrong portion of his earth fill collapsed. This gave him something to do the second day. He redesigned and reconstructed the whole layout.

This second day was also Linc's twelfth birthday, July 27th. Devon baked a chocolate cake and frosted it with chocolate icing. We had birthday candles and balloons and party favors and gifts: a wrist watch and a Boy Scout knife, and a fork and spoon kit, known at once as the Runcible. In the evening a grand performance of caber-tossing preceded the biggest bonfire ever. Nick and Devon were trying to outdo themselves in the sizes of logs they hauled for burning, and, remembering the Scottish games, got inspired to put on a contest. Linc and Brian and I laughed until exhausted as they went wobbling down the beach, balancing their tall awkward poles (cabers) and struggling to heave them in the air so that the caber toppled end over end. All that was missing were the bagpipes. We sat around the fire until late listening to Devon's guitar. It was a grand way to celebrate a boy's birthday.

Thursday was a calm cloudy day, perfect for paddling. Brian regretfully said goodbye to his dam which had failed him again the second night, and we took to the river, keeping close to shore. Eleven miles or so along the way we sighted buildings on the opposite banks, the ones to our left. They looked like they could have been part of an oil exploration camp.

"I think the camp is dead," said someone.

"They wouldn't abandon it with all that equipment around," said someone else.

"Sure they would," a third person broke in. "Remember the dump we saw the last time that was waiting for the barges to haul it away?"

"But there are vehicles here, and that means it's alive."

"I suppose Canol was alive? What about the vehicles there?" The family conference, as you might call it, was in full tilt.

Then someone shouted "Shut up and listen," and we had enough sense to stop our babbling and listen. Sure enough, we heard a generator humming.

"Let's go look!" A lovely suggestion — at once we turned our boats to cross over.

The current was strong but our paddling this time was stronger, and soon we were crossing the shallows to a beach. As we drew nearer we could see the detailed layout of the camp. Two rows of aluminum trailers formed living quarters, mess hall, machine shop, laundry, and storage buildings. To their right stood two Foremost trucks — strange-looking vehicles like large flat-bed trucks only supported by pedestals on top of two sets of cat tracks. To the right was a helicopter, and a great stack of oil drums stood between the buildings and the beach.

As we landed, a man dressed in white T-shirt and white dungarees came from the living quarters to meet us. "You the family from California?" he asked. The river news had included us, and we were expected, in a way. "Come up for coffee as soon as you get settled," he invited.

We carefully beached the boats and tied the painters to large rocks. A tug and barge might pass by and in these shallows the wake could set up waves large enough to wash well up on the shore. When we walked into the mess trailer the man who had greeted us, Charley Vaillancourt, the cook, had laid out five place settings and spread a feast. All that was missing was the coffee! Mr. Vaillancourt apologized, "The barge is due at any minute with the next month's supplies!" Instead, he served us an immense pitcher of hot, delicious tea.

Then he announced, "The laundry and shower room is yours. Everyone is out of camp, and no one will be around for the next hour and a half. You will find soap and towels ready for you — make yourselves at home."

"Can I be first?" I asked, heading for the door. A half hour later the others had their turn. Bush camp was never like this.

Charley excused himself to take a nap, a regular afternoon practice among the cooks of the North. A camp, like an army, runs on its stomach, and the good cook takes his rest during the camp's off hours in order to be ready with the food and drink at 6 a.m., 6 p.m., and 12 midnight if need be. We went from the mess hall to look about the camp, and met next the Camp Manager, Mr. Laurie Baird, and the helicopter pilot, Jerry MacArthur. We learned we were in an exploration camp of the Calgary Geo-Physical Service Corporation. There was a crew of about twenty men who were 'copter-ferried daily into the bush. Here they took seismographic soundings in an attempt to map the land far below the surface of the earth, looking for the contours and the textures that might mean oil. Nick who had been doing research on ultrasonics in his work as a metallurgical engineer, was able to take an intelligent interest in Mr. Baird's description of their project, while all I could manage was the gist of it.

As we stood talking, a large floatplane flew over, circled, and landed. A short time later the barge was sighted upstream and soon made the tricky maneuver around the shallows to the docking place. Now we had a chance to see the Foremost semi-amphibian truck go into operation. It was weird. The tracks swiveled around on their center-post suspension. The truck waddled down the bank, through the creek, up the bank, and out into the river where the floatplane's contents were easily transferred to the truck. Then back it rumbled to the cooking storehouse and the unloading. We learned that this truck is proving to be invaluable in the land of muskeg and permafrost.

An hour had gone by in our touring and talking. We went to our boats and prepared to leave, not wishing to disturb our cook's nap. But before we had launched, Charley appeared with a paper carton of luxuries: two loaves of bread, a can of honey, a can of peanut butter, three cans of salmon, and a pound can of butter. As we left the helicopter took off too. We traveled for twenty more miles before making camp. My log sums it up with two words, "lovely day."

It was well that we enjoyed it, for the next day was something else. My log merely records "family fight."

We had camped that night only a few miles from the deadly Sans Sault Rapids. As far back as Fort Simpson we had been warned of their treachery. Sixty-five miles back at Norman Wells a large sign warns "Dangerous Rapids ahead, 65 miles. Boats are cautioned to keep to the left shore." Lives had been lost by people who had failed to heed this warning, the most recent in 1960. The cook at the oil exploration camp told us there was a memorial shelter on a knoll overlooking the rapids, on the left side. This was the day we were to pass through, but first we wanted to make a brief pilgrimage to the memorial.

A little before noon we spotted the cross atop the aluminum structure and tied our boats while we went to pay our visit. There was no trail. We plowed through the bush and up the mossy hillock to stand at last before the little shelter. Within were two books, wrapped in plastic and placed in a waterproof container. One was a Bible, the other a register which we signed. Also there was a copy of the memorial services, to Hugh Donald Lockhart Gordon, age 21, who made his last camp near this spot the day before he died in Sans Sault Rapids, August 10, 1960. There was his picture too, and the words "He lived only the singing years." My eyes were misty as I turned away and looked across the river where I could see and hear those vicious rapids.

We left the memorial, much quieter than we had arrived, and started our trek back to the boats.

"Don't forget to keep to the left," Nick called to Devon, who had reached his kayak first and shoved off.

Dev did not deign to answer or even show he had heard, being absorbed in private thought of his own. I followed with Brian, then came Nick with Linc.

What happened next was almost too swift to follow. As Devon took the lead, a little shift in current made him take on a burst of speed and swept him a little further toward the right than both Nick and I thought he should be. Because of the variation in current we quickly dropped behind. I tossed a worried look to Nick, and called tentatively "Devon," but Dev did not hear. Immediately Nick let out a bellow that could not be ignored, and with an impatient "Whaddayawant now?" Devon turned his kayak around and marked time. The tone, the tension, the fear all boiled at once in both men, and Nick blew.

"Get in to shore," he roared. "We're going to settle this right now." Absolutely seething, Devon beached and climbed out, and the shouting began in earnest. Brian and I, meanwhile, maintained a discreet distance. We moved in fairly close—I hoped it would soon blow over — but the river was very shallow there so we hung up on a rock about thirty feet from shore and a bit downstream.

"They sure are mad, aren't they?" Brian whispered.

"Don't worry, Son. Let them settle it themselves. They don't need us," I whispered back.

Just about then Devon summed up his point of view, loud and clear, using a few choice expletives. Nick's reaction was instantaneous, unthinking, and direct: with a mighty swoosh of his double-bladed paddle he aimed a blow at his son that should have creamed him proper. But Dev, with the reaction time of a 19-year-old, ducked at the last instant and the blade whizzed over his head, a clean miss, almost throwing Nick on his face. Fortunately for Nick, Dev's dodging caused him to lose his balance and fall into the water or I think he might have clouted Nick with his own paddle.

Meanwhile at the instant Nick swung, something turned me on: I was no longer so convinced "they don't need us."

"Enough!" I roared, and leaped out of the kayak, only to flounder in ice-cold water up to my thighs.

"Knock it off this instant, you two," I continued barking, and splashed toward them. I felt, in spite of the water, as if I were entering the locker room at school trying to break up a row between two students who were about to snatch each other bald headed. Instinctively I reached for the non-existent whistle around my neck.

"Stop it, stop it, stop it!" I kept on shouting and sloshed toward them, afraid that if I shut up they would start in on each other again, but they had long ago stopped at the first yell. They stood there panting and glaring.

"Talk to him," Nick said. "I can't get through to him."

"Talk to him," Dev said. "He won't listen to me."

"No one is going to talk to anyone," said I in my meanest gym teacher voice, almost adding "or I'll haul you both up to the dean." Instead I decreed "We are all going to have a five-minute cooling off period and No One Is to Say One Word to Anyone."

"Grumble, grumble," they started.

"NO ONE — FIVE MINUTES!"

I had spoken.

They didn't quite cower. I guess the logic came through. In silence I started gathering wood. Brian and Linc, the non-combatants, picked up their cues and brought more. A fire soon was going, and the younger boys brought the lunches from the kayaks. In silence I led Devon to one side of the fire, then started to dry myself on the other side, near my husband. Quietly pieces of food were handed around. Just as quietly pieces of shattered personalities were being assembled again. In those few minutes Nick released his last hold on Devon's childhood and Devon assumed his position in the family as a grown man.

"I'm sorry," one of them said.

"I'm sorry too," said the other.

The two shook hands. The younger boys exchanged looks and smiled a little. I stepped out of the locker room.

13 «

THE RAMPARTS

Far to the right the rapids surged and roared, the sound grew louder and louder as we made our swift passage on their left flank. Here the river measured two miles wide. One set of rapids started flush with the bank and extended across the stream over a quarter of a mile. An overlapping second set began about three-quarters of a mile later and was almost a mile in width. There was no room or time to change direction once our course was set. We chose the only safe channel, the mild calm waters to the left, and the current did the rest. These rapids are an extension of a rocky limestone ridge which rises to the east 1000 to 1700 feet high. During high water four-foot waves bound from the boulder-strewn river bed, reaching heights of eight feet during low water. They are considered totally impassable; no one has ever shot them successfully.

Once the rapids end, an island divides the river into two navigable channels, the current drops to five miles per hour. At the upriver tip of this island the tug *Sans Sault* together with barges and a dredge, is anchored. We bent our paddles to pass on the right of the island and visit the crew of this dredging operation.

The captain, Len McKinley, met us as we came aboard.

"Well, I see you made it," he said using the understated greeting we had come to recognize as standard among the many people who were keeping an eye open for us. "Cook will have supper for you as soon as the crew is done with theirs."

After supper we had a guided tour with the skipper. The outfit consisted of the tugboat, a dredge, a gravel barge, a supply barge, a mess-hall barge, and a barracks barge. About a dozen barge men and four tugboat crewmen plus the captain

119

and the cook worked on the project which was deepening the main channel through the Sans Sault passage. Several years had already been spent on it, and the job was not yet done, but when it is completed, ocean-going vessels of considerable draft will be able to come upriver instead of transferring supplies to barges. The working season is short, and the rock is hard, but life on the project is pleasant enough, albeit lonely. Each two weeks the tug takes the crewmen to Norman Wells for a break. After the brief season is over it's Outside to the bright lights again for most of them, with plenty of pay saved and an adventurous summer to recall.

"Thank you, Captain McKinley," Linc and Brian said as they dashed down the gangplank to shore.

"We shall never forget your hospitality," Nick echoed as he and Devon and I followed.

"Take care," he replied. "Keep to the right channel for the next two miles. Have a good trip."

The men stood on deck, smiling and calling to us, some taking pictures. In just a few minutes we were away, fairly flying in the five-mile-an-hour current. We rounded a bend and they were out of sight.

The hours passed and the swift current continued. We moved to the left of the river. One of our regular pastimes when the water was smooth was to see how close we could come to swimming water fowl before scaring them into flight. In the late afternoon this day we had been amusing ourselves again with this game. Now Devon started toward a bird floating near the left shore, and the rest of us followed. Closer and closer we came, but the creature did not fly.

"What is it?" Linc called.

The bird was about the size of a small duck.

"It's a baby Checkered Loon!" Dev answered. "He's too young to fly yet."

Closer and closer we moved. Now the bird was swimming frantically, but we were overtaking it. Suddenly, noiselessly, he slipped under the water.

"Look!" called Dev, "I can follow his bubbles."

The Foremost truck is dwarfed by the bush cargo plane as it backs under a wing, preparatory to loading supplies for the exploration camp. There are no wharves or floating docks here but because the river makes a wide sweep the water is extremely shallow. The floatplane must beware of sandbars in landing and taking off.

Modern transport is a big problem in the Far North. Extreme winter cold and partly thawed summer ground make conventional freighting impossible. The truck shown, called a Foremost, is semi-amphibian and was designed to operate in tundra, muskeg, and permafrost.

Below the Sans Sault Rapids the Department of Public Works tug, *Sans Sault*, nestles against the crewman's mess-hall barge. Also shown are the dredge, two storage barges, and a rock-hauling barge. Theirs is a work season of no more than two months for the ice starts forming in September and does not leave until mid-June.

Like a long string of boxcars the trailers sit in two rows to form a snug settlement for a seismographic oil seeking crew. When a campsite is changed these buildings are hauled on skids and moved on barges—a regular summertime activity.

A baby Checkered Arctic Loon. Too young to fly, he was chased down by our kayaks and held captive only long enough for this photograph.

Sure enough, a trail of tiny bubbles gave the inexperienced fledgling away. In about a minute he surfaced, and there we were, still right with him.

Now began a chase that the little creature had to lose. We surrounded him. Shorter and shorter were his underwater swims. Tighter and tighter drew the triangle of boats around him. At last he could dive no more. He swam to Devon's kayak and bravely pecked at the side of the boat. Quietly Dev watched the desperate little bird. Then, as he drifted closer, Dev, with a swift motion scooped him up in his hands and held him gently but firmly out of the water.

"Isn't he beautiful!" breathed the boys. The soft grey markings stood out clear and bright. The droplets of water on him glistened in the sunshine.

"Sh! Sh! Don't scare him," I cautioned unnecessarily.

We were all speaking in whispers.

Nick had his camera out and in the twilight attempted some pictures. Then, when we had all admired enough, Devon gently placed the loon in the water and we sat still and watched.

The bird swam a little, looked over his shoulder and emitted the saddest sound, almost like the cooing of a mourning dove. Then he swam sturdily toward shore as we drifted away.

Now we let the current carry us, keeping only far enough from the 100-foot-steep clay banks to avoid the back eddies. For the most part we were quiet, and were treated to a symphony of bird calls. At one spot we heard the patter of falling pebbles and dug in our paddles to stop our progress and watch a huge porcupine scrabble in panic up the bank away from us. We helped him along with hoots.

This sound, we discovered, started more pebbles falling, so we continued our drifting with occasional whoops, starting minor landslides for our amusement. No one was hungry enough to stop. We nibbled peanuts and candy from a lunch, dipped water from the river for a gin and orange juice, and continued our drifting until midnight when we camped at last.

Our next day, Saturday, July 30th, was beautiful, calm, bright, and warm. We crossed the river to our right, making our own uncharted track through sandbars and past low grassy islands, going six miles downstream before reaching the main banks. Devon, who was in the lead, suddenly started a wild wig-wag with his arms. He was just about to pass the point of a long skinny island, the last one between us and shore. We interpreted his signals as:

"Quiet! I see a creature on the banks."

Quickly, silently we paddled to him. As our line of sight coincided with his we could see the cause of his excitement: a bear stood in the grass, browsing, unaware of the audience. We steered closer and closer. But we were seen, or heard, or smelled, or all three, for with a snort the bear ran into the bush. We had been thinking about lunching there, but not knowing how far the bear might have run we decided to move on.

Now we kept only a very few feet from shore, scanning the bush for any other sign of wildlife. In just a few minutes we saw a duck swimming ahead of us. She spotted us and at once began to flop oddly in the water.

"I'll be darned," Nick observed.

"The wounded duck act!" Devon joined in.

We were all immediately on the alert for her ducklings. Sure enough, by peering carefully along the shoreline we finally saw them, four of them. Too young to fly yet, they blended so perfectly with the muddy banks that even on our films it is almost impossible to pick them out. Our presence was a great harassment to mother duck and children, but we stared and chased to our hearts' content, then continued our search for a lunch spot.

Afterwards we paddled and drifted to the mouth of the Tsintu River, near the head of the Ramparts, and there we camped.

When I look back on our trip I still recall the effortless drifting sessions with a touch of incredulity. This afternoon, when we drifted, we maintained a distance of twenty to fifty feet from shore. The three boats were tenuously rafted together by paddles and painters. Folded sweatshirts made our pillows.

Field glasses were propped on stomachs for instantaneous use if needed.

Never in my adult life have I ever had enough time or opportunity simply to lie supine, watching the clouds roll by. Here, sprawled out in the gently moving kayak — which, by the way, kept up a very slow constant rotation as it drifted along — I could see clouds, treetops, banks, water, just by lowering an eyelid. If I lowered the eyelid enough, I was rocked into the best of catnaps by the gentlest of lullabies: the soft sounds of wavelets on the kayak's hull.

Walt Whitman wrote in his *Children of Adam,*

"All things please the soul, but these please the soul well." I wish I'd said that.

The last morning of July, a Sunday, found us only 15 miles from Fort Good Hope, but with the exciting stretch of river called the Ramparts lying between us and our goal. Here the river narrows from approximately three miles to a quarter of a mile wide, and limestone cliffs rising from 100 to 200 feet on either side line a channel over seven miles long. The current climbs to six and seven miles per hour and rapids lie at the Ramparts' entrance. On a quiet day during the mid-summer season this strip of river presents only an exciting challenge, but we woke to a day of wind, so had an element of hazard added.

"Keep to the right," we admonished one another, but as we approached the Ramparts' mouth we found it impossible to follow this sound advice. A north wind was blowing, and high waves came rolling in on our port side. Farther and farther to our left we moved in order to keep from broaching. Even so, we shipped a hatful of water from time to time, and had some thoroughly wet seats from sitting in two inches of water in the boats before the current carried us far enough downstream for the cliffs to cut off the wind. Then, little by little, we moved to the right side of the river, alternately steering and bailing.

Nick saw a tiny gravel shingle at the base of one of the cliffs, and called, "Let's stop and dry out."

I could not see where we would find any wood, but the stop sounded fine so I agreed. To my surprise, by scouting carefully we found enough wood for a very satisfactory fire to dry our wet "bums," as the Canadians call them.

The cliffs above us made the nesting place for hundreds of swallows. As we ate lunch we watched the endless comings and goings of these birds. Lincoln, the bird watcher of the family, organized a walk which took the hikers very close to the nests. I organized myself on a life jacket pillow by the fire and took a nap. At last we returned to our boats again for the last of the paddle to Fort Good Hope.

A half hour later we started to round the gentle turn which gave us our first sight of the town. There, like an immense frosted birthday cake, the white painted red-roofed buildings gleamed in the sun, the distortion of six miles' distance playing odd optical games with our delighted eyes. The current now had dropped from six to three miles per hour so we knew we had almost two hours to go. We cast one last look over our shoulders at the picturesque Indian camp far behind us near the left opening of the Ramparts, now disappearing as we completed rounding the turn, then plied our paddles for the long pull to town.

"I wonder if we'll make some more friends here," said the younger boys.

"I wonder if our Fort Norman mail has caught up with us," said Devon.

"I wonder if the Hudson's Bay man will open the store on Sunday," I said.

"I wonder what news we'll hear about Duc Meyer from the Mounties," said Nick.

So, absolutely filled with wonder, we toiled along our way.

14 «
FORT GOOD HOPE

Fort Good Hope! Where does the name come from? I never thought to ask. Scattered out over two hilltops with a little valley between, and the Jackfish Creek cutting in on its northwest side, this village is home to perhaps a hundred Indian families and a handful of whites. There is a post office, a government radio and meteorological station, a Roman Catholic mission, a nursing station, an elementary school, a Hudson's Bay store, and a Royal Canadian Mounted Police detachment. We secured our boats at a floating dock near the entrance of the creek and prepared to walk up a road to the town proper, high on an eighty-foot bank. It had taken us nine days to travel the seventy miles from Norman Wells. We knew that our stay could only be overnight. We hoped it would be an interesting one.

Just before docking, a motorboat with two Indian youths came by. One boy was holding a walkie-talkie radio. On impulse Nick picked up his transceiver, pulled up the aerial, and whispered, "Hello, hello."

The Indian appeared to listen, then he tried to send a message. Nick listened intently. Nothing. At the same instant, in the same motion, boy and man reached up and shoved their retractable aerials back into place, then made the universal gesture of hands spread, shoulders shrugged. Different frequencies. Laughter from us all, then the motorboat passed by.

Now we walked up the steep roadway for our first close view of town. From a distance it had looked immense, like a city. Here we could see it was just a tiny village, very old in places, very new in others, almost an anachronistic combination of nineteenth and twentieth century living. We walked on a narrow board sidewalk past the Roman Catholic church on our right and the rectory on our left. Above our heads power lines indicated an electric supply, but in front of us a huge stack of corded wood told where these two buildings got their heat. Further down the street we came to a string of Indian cabins which were all made of unpainted hand-hewn logs, squared by hand, mud chinked, and very old. Their windows were small and aslant and each cabin had a single door, well shimmed but still hanging out of plumb. No grass or flowers grew around these simple homes. Directly across the street were the white picket fences of the trim white Royal Canadian Mounted Police dwelling, a modern home surrounded by lawn, flying the Canadian maple leaf flag from a tall flagpole set in a rock-trimmed flower garden.

We turned in here to report to the Mountie, and to ask about a place to camp. We found the duty station "manned" by Mrs. John Hayes, the wife of the Mountie in charge, and her small son and daughter. Mr. Hayes had flown out that morning on a mission and would not be back for two days. Mrs. Hayes, however, was well up to her duties.

"John will be so sorry to miss you," she said. "You may camp in the compound by the jail, and use the facilities next to the building."

The jail house, we discovered, was the attractive little cottage right across the lawn from her home. Later that afternoon we were told rather proudly by the young son, age about four, that "My daddy puts the drunk men in the jail, and they use that bathroom next door."

Mrs. Hayes also showed us the long, steep, wooden staircase which led down to the Royal Canadian Mounted Police dock, where we could beach our boats. We left the younger boys with instructions to meet us at the dock while we walked back to the wharf to bring the kayaks along.

Little by little the camp chores were done. The tents were up, the cooking equipment ready, the clothing bags and reading supplies in their places. Devon was commissioned to look for the Hudson's Bay man, and the boys were freed to roam and "make some friends." I went with Nick to the shoreline again to help lift a boat from the water and look for a leak.

We noticed far down the beach, between two and three hundred yards off, a rather large group of Indians just sitting on the banks looking across the river as if waiting for something. We looked too, and listened, and soon heard, then saw, a large floatplane approaching. In a few moments it landed, taxied up to another floating dock below the watching people, and discharged about a dozen natives who were warmly greeted by their friends and relatives. We left off our staring and started the back-bending task of lifting the kayak from the water.

A folding Klepper kayak when empty weighs about 75 pounds. There was perhaps another 25 pounds of equipment still in the boat we were handling—easy enough to move for a short distance, but the rocks were unsteady, the grip awkward. I concentrated on my end of the boat and gave a mighty heave. At once I knew something was wrong. I looked up to see what Nick was doing at his end of the boat, and there he was, seated in the water with his end of the boat in his lap! He did not look the slightest bit amused.

Meekly I asked, "Did I do that?"

Firmly he answered, "You did," then struggled to his feet and picked up his end of the boat again.

I didn't even say, "I'm sorry." In truth, I didn't dare. Together this time we brought the kayak out of the water, then turned it over, keel up, and made the long wordless climb to the campsite. I left Nick looking for some dry clothes and went to the Royal Canadian Mounted Police house to see about drinking water. Here I found Mrs. Hayes preparing supper and chuckling quietly over some news her little son had brought her. When she saw me she told me her boy had just come in, all agog, to report:

"That lady just threw her daddy in the river!"

About this time Nick, changed and dry and puffing happily on a cigarette, came in and we repeated the news to him. He shouted with laughter. It was then I told him "I'm sorry!"

From here we went to find Devon at the Bay where Mr. Cormack, the Factor, was just opening the store for him.

"Do we have any mail?" I asked anxiously.

"Oh, yes," he replied, "a big stack."

Mr. Cormack was a tall, grey-haired, very scrubbed appearing man in, perhaps, his late sixties. His voice was soft, the accent clipped. He led us to the mail section of the store and placed a dozen letters in our hands, including those from Fort Norman that the stranger on the beach had forgotten to bring us in Norman Wells. We bought some canned foods and walked back home to prepare an easy dinner.

While eating, we heard the unmistakable sound of a chain saw. Across the street beside one of the extremely old log cabins were two teenage Indians, a boy and a girl, operating it. They were dressed like high school boys and girls in the States: jeans, sneakers, bright tops, and went about their work of cutting a half dozen or so sticks of firewood. Then the boy turned off the saw, thrust it underneath the house, and the two of them left. At this moment a tiny elderly Indian woman, wearing a traditional long print dress and mukluks, emerged from the door of the house, walked to the new pile of wood with the little hesitant steps of the aged, picked up an armful, then disappeared into the house only to reappear and to repeat the process again and again until the wood was all safely tucked inside. We longed to take her picture, but did not know how to approach her without intruding on her privacy and, perhaps, offending her.

After dinner we met Mrs. Roy Corless, the young wife of a local contractor. Mr. Corless too was out of town on business, so she and the Mountie's wife were sharing their evening meal. Mrs. Corless, who lived at the opposite end of town, invited us to end our evening walk at her house for a cup of coffee and some cake.

The two boys ran on ahead to play with some Indian boys they had already met, and Nick and Devon and I went on a stroll through town. One of the places we visited was the Roman Catholic church. The outside was extremely plain, almost severe, but inside the sanctuary was painted with primitive splendor. Many an hour of loving, painstaking care had been spent in covering every surface of walls, rafters, and ceiling with pictures and designs in vivid color. Some Far

Interior view of Roman Catholic Church in Fort Good Hope, photographed by Thomy Nilsson and sent to the family after they had returned home.

At a summer fish camp Mrs. Williams, a Loucheaux Indian, prepares part of the ton of whitefish required to feed her husband's dog team during the winter. The drying rack is in the background.

At Fort Good Hope, on the steps of the town jail, Lincoln (center) and Brian (far right) pose with their favorite Indian friends.

A hockey game gets under way in Fort Good Hope's main street. Brian is in the center, fourth from the left. Lincoln is at the far right. The other children are Slavey Indian boys; most girls this age remained indoors and made no attempt to meet the white strangers.

North artist had done panels for the Stations of the Cross, and at the entrance of the church two large paintings by an Oblate Father related the whole structure to the setting. One picture showed a sunrise service, attended by Indians, presided over by a black-cassocked priest, and watched through the open door of a cabin by a bedridden Oblate Father. The other might well have been titled "Our Lady of the Ramparts." It portrayed a vision of Mary standing above the picturesque fish camp at the head of the Ramparts as seen by an Indian woman and man in a canoe.

How I wished we had been carrying flash equipment! The only picture we could take of this chapel would be the one in our memories.

Now we walked back to the main section of town and found a vigorous hockey game in progress. Brian and Lincoln, together with about twenty boys of their age, were enmeshed in one of the wildest fracases I have ever seen. There were two ice hockey sticks, a couple of plain sticks, and one plastic ball for equipment. The teams were flexible, or so it seemed, boys changing sides at will. Whoever had possession of a stick had the right to use it on the ball if he could, but anyone else had the right to wrest a stick away from him and use it himself. It was wild! I never did learn where the goals were. I found out later that the game went all over town, including through the jail yard, down to the beach, and back again. As we passed by Nick and I could not bear to look at the wildly flailing sticks and those kids who were literally whooping around "like Indians."

Instead we got started in a conversation with an Indian couple, Mr. and Mrs. Eddy Cook, as they stood in front of their home. One of their younger sons was in the hockey game. Mr. Cook was particularly proud of his eldest son who was apparently a fine athlete. This boy, who was not in town today, would be at Inuvik in high school this year, and there was hope that he would some day have a career in professional sports. The Cooks knew that education would open doors for their boy. They had lived and worked among the white men so that they were not so shy and talked quite freely.

From here we started down the hill, past the Hudson's Bay store, past another series of native dwellings, and stopped to look briefly at a strange sight. It looked as if a very long building had just collapsed in a heap in the creek at the foot of the hill. All that showed was one hundred and fifty feet of peaked roof. Subsequently we learned that the townspeople had made a great community effort to build, cooperatively, a curling rink. The creek running by was a perfect site, for curling requires a frozen ice surface. Although the building was soon completed, enough attention had not been paid to adequate bracing, so unfortunately, the first windstorm of any size flattened the building, but luckily, no one was inside at the time. Little by little the wood was disappearing — probably as fuel.

Up the next hill we walked toward the contractor's home and the school ground. The homes here were new, still of log construction, but very recently built. In the yards of almost all of them dogs were staked out who watched us solemnly. Each home also had a square cast-iron stove in its yard: summertime is no time to cook indoors. Also gleaming white enameled washing machines stood in the yards of many houses. Passing by another cabin we noticed dog harnesses hanging on pegs in the front wall of the house, and in the back a Honda motor scooter was parked. Further up the hill we came upon a group of Indian men sitting in the warm evening sunshine on the porch of a cabin.

We smiled and Nick called, "Good evening."

They smiled back. "Hello," they said.

Then one of the men asked Nick, "Say, what happened down there at the river?"

We stopped walking. Nick looked hard at the men, then at me. I pantomimed shoving him in the water, and we all exploded into laughter. Then I stood by, making myself be quiet, while the men talked. I guess everyone of them at some time or another had been dunked one way or another in the river. Nick's experience, albeit uniquely brought about, made him one of them.

We walked up to the top of the hill and looked out over the schoolyard to the school building and to the teacher's house. Here we saw a third kind of log cabin construction called Pan-Abode. This is a method of building in which the logs are routed and shaped almost in a tongue and groove construction, making a weathertight structure that needs no chinking. It is a recent development, adapting and modernizing an ancient and almost forgotten Scandinavian skill, only very recently introduced to the Far North. Special tools are needed to dress the logs, but there seems to be a real future in Pan-Abode cabins.

Now we turned back to Mrs. Corless' home and spent an hour of cake, coffee, and talk. Mr. Corless is a general contractor and, like the free trader of Fort Providence, and the tugboat owner of Fort Simpson, he has found his fortune and his freedom in the Northwest Territories. We left Mrs. Corless after 11:00 p.m., carrying a loaf of her delicious home-baked bread for our breakfast. The younger boys were still involved in the hockey game, but almost willingly came when we called on our way by. As soon as they left, the game dissolved and the other boys went home. It made us wonder if, perhaps, there had been special concessions granted by the Indian children's parents in allowing their game to continue so late because of visitors there. We didn't speculate too long. We were thankful for no broken heads or arms or noses or fingers, and dropped into bed wearily.

That night the town noises were so different from the bush noises that I did not fall to sleep very soon. About 1:00 a.m., just as I was dropping off, I was treated to a phenomenon of sound that Mrs. Hayes had warned us about. On the other side of the R.C.M.P. station stood a large kennel and run holding about eighteen Mountie sled dogs, most of them huskies and malemutes. Every night at approximately 1:00 a.m. these dogs howl along with every other dog in town. The howling usually starts with a dog over on the school side of town, or perhaps with a wolf out in the bush. But once that first howl is heard the dogs take up the cry and pass it along until the whole town is serenaded. Then, after a few minutes, it stops completely. Not barking, understand, but a mournful lost-soul howling such as you only hear in movies or in your imagination.

Mrs. Hayes said she sleeps right through it now, although the kennels are just outside her bedroom window. I have a notion that if some night the dogs did not set off their noise on schedule she would wake up with a start and cry out "What was that?"

As the dogs' voices faded away, I drifted into sleep.

In the morning, later than usual, we broke our camp and carried our belongings to the beach. The younger boys found their six or seven favorite Indian friends, and soon became engrossed in play. We started over to the Bay for final purchases when Nick turned to Dev and me, and said,

"You know, I'd forgot. Mr. Cormack is an old friend of Angus Sherwood's. We were supposed to bring him greetings."

We had indeed forgotten. During the years when Angus was a free trader, Mr. Cormack had been his business competitor. All rivals during the working day, they were cordial friends during the evenings. It had been a long time since their last reunion but the ties were still there. When we entered the store, Nick delivered his message.

How sorry I was we had not remembered the night before! Much of Mr. Cormack's diffidence evaporated. We were introduced a little later to Mrs. Cormack. Talk went smoothly, and with a sense of ease. I was impressed again by what the sharing of a friend can do in making a new acquaintance.

During the last part of the morning we had coffee with Mrs. Hayes. She greeted us with welcome news.

"I just got word from Fort Norman that your friend, Duc Meyer, left there this morning," she told us.

This was exciting and meant that at the rate he was traveling, Duc would overtake us before we reached the delta. We would have to start keeping watch for him.

We gave Mrs. Hayes our estimated time of arrival at the next check point, Arctic Red River, two hundred miles away. Then we rounded up Lincoln and Brian whom we found with a group of Indian boys squatted in a circle apparently playing some kind of game involving pebbles. Down to the beach we marched, followed by the chattering group. Mrs. Hayes and her two children sat at the top of the steps and waved farewell.

At last the goodbyes were said, the final handshakes exchanged, and we were waterborne again. The young boys called out to their friends,

"Don't forget, no more than three to a boat."

"O.K. — see you — so long," they called back, then crouched down again in a tight circle with their small stones in the center. We could see them gesturing and hear them chattering as we moved away downstream.

"What was that all about?" Nick asked as we picked up speed.

"Oh, we gave them a riddle," said Brian.

"The one about the cannibals and the missionaries," Linc added.

Devon took over. "You know. The three cannibals and three missionaries come to a river and want to cross over. They only have a dugout canoe, and it will hold only three at the most. Or is it two? Anyway, you can never have two cannibals with one missionary at any time or they will eat the missionary. How do they cross?"

"Did you get the answer?" Nick asked.

"No. In fact, we're not even sure we remembered the riddle correctly," answered Dev.

"Sounds great," I said, "particularly when you consider that much of the early settling up here was promoted by missionaries. The schoolmaster will be quite surprised to come back from vacation and find his boys puzzling over cannibals and missionaries crossing rivers if they don't figure it out and have to ask him."

"He'll be more than quite surprised," Dev replied. "In fact, he ought to have a real interesting social studies lesson on his hands."

"How do you figure?" Nick asked.

"Well," the boys interrupted, "We told them the cannibals· and missionaries and their dugout canoe were crossing the Mississippi River."

15 «

REUNION

This was the day we had been waiting for: the day we were to cross the Arctic Circle. We meant to celebrate, but unfortunately for our plans we really didn't know exactly where the imaginary line was. No indication showed on the river charts and we had forgotten the exact latitude as stated in our geography books back home. But we had heard figures varying from "eight to fourteen" miles beyond Good Hope, so when we had gone twenty miles we made our camp.

The site was breathtakingly beautiful; above us loomed a shale cliff with undersized trees and bushes in niches up its face as though landscaped for an "art and garden" show. At its base sparkled a creek from a miniature waterfall. The shingled beach, both sand and shale, abounded in weather-polished driftwood logs. All town noises were gone; we were back in our beloved bush.

Bush life is prized among the people of this country. Town, with all its many attractions, cannot be put down, but the call of the hunting camp and fish camp compels attention too. Many natives can hold regular jobs for months at a time, but when the brief summer comes they find the nine-to-five grind too much for them, and take to the bush until winter. After six weeks on the river we understood and agreed with their thinking.

That night, as I prepared a magnificent dinner of beef Stroganoff, Nick called out,

"Hey, Honey, look at Devon and the boys."

I had sent them to the creek for water but they decided that for the Arctic Circle Camp only pure waterfall water would do, so they organized themselves into the Arctic Beaver Patrol with Devon, the Eagle Scout, leading Second Class Linc

134

and Tenderfoot Brian for the purpose of engineering a log bridge across the creek near the falls. Once it was bridged the three started an elaborate tightrope showoff as they approached the falls, scooped the water and passed the bucket back to shore. Pirouettes, arabesques, chassés, all were made into an elegant routine. It went on and on.

Nick and I were particularly pleased to watch Dev's involvement with his brothers. We felt Dev's position on our vacation to be the most difficult of all. A ten-year-old and an eleven-year-old are still pretty much at ease with their parents, and they have each other for companionship however much they bicker. But a young man of nineteen misses youthful talk and action. It was fun to see Dev being a boy again, or at least acting the counselor's role with his brothers as he had the previous summer with other children at a private camp. We sipped our gin and juice and watched the performance.

At last dinner was ready, and Nick shouted, "Come and get it, boys."

They pranced over, passing the water bucket daintily between them.

"Almost time to add the sour cream," I said. "It's beef Stroganoff tonight."

"Please!" replied Devon, in the phoniest of Italian accents. "Not Stroganoff. It's 'Stroganini.' We are the Flying Spumonis," he announced, "World's greatest aerialists in the art of fallen-log-walking. I am Luigi Spumoni. And here is my brother Giovanni and my brother Pietro."

The two boys bowed elaborately.

"Stroganini it is," I replied, "In honor of the Spumoni Brothers' Exclusive Arctic Appearance."

Luigi, Giovanni, and Pietro indicated approval of the change, then watched as the dehydrated sour cream was reconstituted with their special waterfall water and added to the Stroganoff. With many an appreciative murmur the plates were filled. Applesauce, fresh biscuits and butter completed the main course, gingerbread was ready for dessert.

Luigi Spumoni spoke, with a sigh, "If only we had some good red vino to go with our Stroganoff, I mean Stroganini."

I took his cue. "Ah yes! If only we had some wine!"

Nick, who had heard this type of conversation before, paid scant attention but did sigh "Mmm."

"Dev" I said, "why don't you go on a search for some. Maybe you could trample out some berries or something."

"Very well, mother dear, I shall." He reached behind him and opened the case in which we carried our fishing equipment and which he had removed from his boat while Nick was busy elsewhere. Feeling down inside the case he pulled out a bottle of Canadian Claret and gave it to his astonished dad.

"Where in the world did you? . . ." Nick began.

We all sat and smirked.

"How long have you? . . ." he went on.

We mugged and rolled our eyes. Finally I told him, "I sneaked it at Norman Wells the second night and we've been hiding it ever since!"

We filled our coffee cups to the brim and proposed toasts to the Arctic, the Flying Spumonis, the Mackenzie, and our-selves in general. At last we had to stop the celebration, but not before the boys had composed a note for the wine bottle and hurled it far out into the river.

"What do you think of the frozen Arctic?" Nick asked the boys.

"It's hot, that's what!" they replied, as they climbed into their down beds, leaving off their pajama tops and not zipping shut the sleeping bags.

"Well, one of these days the weather will be changing," said Nick, but we couldn't really imagine it. The date was only August first.

Next morning the wind had shifted and was coming from the south. This meant thunderstorms, but it also meant great paddling with a helping wind. Around 5:30 the threat of rain drove us to camp. Here we met a peculiar problem. The beach was most inviting, but the approach was through extremely shallow water. Even though our boats had a draft of only a few inches we hung up on the muddy bottom. When we took off our footwear to climb out and pull the boats we sank into black mud almost to our knees. The suction of the mud on the boats was such that we were afraid some of our patches would be pulled off. We tugged and hauled anyway, for rain was imminent, and reached the beach where we found a lovely campsite. Dinner, eaten inside the tent while it rained, made us feel on top again.

When the rain shower was over, Devon led the boys in a commemorative project, still not quite satisfied with the celebration of the night before. First they drew a line in the sand, from the shore to the edge of the bush, and labeled it "Artic Circle," scrawling the two-foot-high letters in the sand on either side of the line. Then they took a small yellow pennant we had made at home with the legend "Nickerson, Alamo, Calif., U.S.A." printed on it. They attached the pennant to a tall slender pole, then propped the pole with rocks and logs beside the, to us, official Arctic Circle.

"There," said Devon, "that's more like it."

Suddenly he spotted something on the ground. With a chuckle he pounced on it and came up with a tiny beetle.

"Proof!" he chortled. "My Teaching Assistant in entomology last term said that this type of chrysomelid beetle was only found north of the Artic Circle, and here the little monster is twenty inches from our line."

"Proof, indeed," I said, "but your spelling is awful."

"Merely authentic, Mom. Nobody in the Arctic ever speaks of anything but the 'Artic'."

He was right. We had even fallen into the habit ourselves. So we let the spelling stand.

As we admired the more formal dedication to our historic passage, we heard the sound of a tugboat and turned to look downstream. In a short time a very small tug appeared, and set its course quite near us.

"Do you suppose they see our flag?" asked Devon.

"Probably." Nick said.

"I hope they don't think it's a distress signal," I fussed.

"Do we have to take it down?" asked the boys.

"No. let's look real casual and unworried," I suggested.

So there we stood, sipping our dinner coffee, peering at the tug through field glasses, and looking casual and unworried.

After a bit the tug gave seven blasts on its whistle, then moved away upstream. The river curved and the boat was soon out of sight, but the sound of its motors ceased abruptly, and we wondered what had happened.

During the night the river dropped, leaving us a fifty-foot strip of black, sticky, gooey mud to traverse with all our equipment. Such a suction was created by the stuff that we could not load the kayaks nearer shore. Loaded close in, the boats simply could not be moved. By the time we were afloat and away we were pretty grumpy, but the magic of the river and the beauty of the scenery worked on us and before long we were cheerful again. This was the day we paddled and drifted a full 25 miles at the edge of quiet rain showers. The cloud formations were, again, magnificent. The showers were heading across the river, sometimes in front of us, sometimes in back of us. By being very quiet and listening carefully we could even hear the rain. Once we heard a different sort of hiss and whisper, and deduced that the rain curtain was headed directly for us. We bent to our paddles and got only the edge of the shower, then drifted and watched it pass away. Little or no wind accompanied these curtains, a phenomenon never observed before and never repeated on this trip.

When the time came to look for a campsite we pulled for the right-hand shore. As we skirted a little island we saw on the mainland a huge black bear and twin cubs browsing in the grass. The slight breeze was toward us, so we were able to creep to within fifty yards of shore before the mother bear sensed danger. The cubs, who had been rolling and frisking about, ran to either side of the mother as she reared up on her hind legs, a good seven feet tall, her head swiveling back and forth. Then she dropped to her feet and ran to the brush, her cubs tightly beside her, and disappeared.

We went about one more mile before making camp at another attractive site. A lovely clear stream entered the river so close to the kitchen area that I could fill the water bucket by taking about three steps. A little further downstream a natural basin said "bathtub" to me, so after dinner I took a bath. The water felt as if it was all of 33 degrees, but I learned long ago in camping that for me there is only one way to wash in cold water: soap from head to toe, then get in and rinse or be forced to wear a coating of dried soapsuds all day. Strangely enough, after the initial numbing the water feels quite nice. Some day I even hope to sell the rest of the family on skinny-dipping, but this evening I was the only bather.

Later that night we sighted another bear and cub walking on the beach about a quarter of a mile upstream from our tent. Brian at once began building a warning system, one that Rube Goldberg would have been proud of. I can't remember exactly what kneebone was connected to which thighbone, but the ultimate was a boulder poised to drop on a snooping bear's head, and the bait was a two-inch piece of bacon rind. We built up the fire before retiring, and I gave Nick's rifle an extra pat before going to sleep, but the bears stayed away so far as we knew. However, in the morning there were fresh tracks in the mud along the edge of the creek farthest from our camp.

On this day we went another 25 miles in superb weather, all threats of storm gone. About lunchtime we came to an abandoned Hudson's Bay trading post, and stopped to explore and reconstruct history for ourselves. We walked across a wide sandy beach, then up the bank about forty feet to where we could see two cabins, one which had been the trader's home, the other the store itself. The cabins were tiny, and while picturesque, no longer habitable. A few articles were strewn about, including some invoices made out to B. Fischer, Hudson's Bay Company, and dated 1934. Some of the walls had been papered with newspapers, which also bore 1934 dates. I sat in a broken rocking chair and looked back up the river, trying to imagine life here as the trader's wife only a generation ago. I could see the native canoes pulled up on the beach, but then my imagination got mixed up with bead-trading scenes from my fourth-grade history books, showing Columbus dealing with the Indians, and I had to give it up.

We looked through two smaller cabins that could not be seen from the beach, probably storehouses of some kind. Altogether, except for the lovely view, this was a dreary place. We were happy to return to the beach for lunch, and soon were on the river again.

The next morning, our fifth since leaving Fort Good Hope, we saw by the map that we were only a few miles from a place called Little Chicago. Probably we never asked the right people, but nobody had any idea where it got its name. The trading post had been abandoned in 1958, and there was some question as to how many people were living at the townsite — a few Indian families, perhaps. There was also an oil-drilling camp nearby, but it was supposed to be deactivated now. We didn't know what we might find, but we decided to keep toward the right-hand shore and look for Little Chicago, and hoped we would not miss it.

There was no need to worry. As we came around the curve of the river the oil camp loomed from the top of a 75-foot bank. Our ears picked up the sound of a generator, our field glasses showed a motorboat moored at the dock, and we knew the place was "live." We steered across a huge contrary backwater, Nick and Devon taking a long lead while I fussed with my camera. As the men neared the dock a figure appeared at the top of the bank where the bulldozed road curved down to the beach. He turned suddenly and ran back into the building near him. Then he reappeared and ran to the dock, waving his arms vigorously. There he stood waiting for the first two kayaks. I could see him talking animatedly to the men.

For a moment I had the irrational thought, "Maybe they've got the plague up there and he's warning us off."

But the next moment Nick and Devon had tied their boats and disembarked. Then I had to put down my camera and grab my paddle because we had been caught by the back eddy and were rapidly being swept upstream! By the time I reached the dock, the others were walking around on shore. Brian and I climbed over the wobbly boards and looked up to see a second man driving a forklift truck down the hill. He swung the forks over to a large wooden pallet, scooped it up, then came down to where we were standing.

"Climb on," he said. "This is the only operating vehicle in camp. I'll drive you up the hill."

The six of us stood on the pallet, clutching one another, talking at the tops of our voices to drown out the truck, thoroughly enjoying that crazy ride up the hill. Soon we were seated inside the mess hall, breathless and laughing over our reception.

Our hosts were Barry Armstrong of Red Deer, Alberta and Clint Campbell of Edmonton.

"We heard you were coming," Clint said, "but we thought you had already passed us by."

"When we saw you, we were afraid maybe you wouldn't stop," continued Barry. "Aren't you hungry? We can't cook, but we have everything."

"How about some steak?" asked Clint.

"Mr. Campbell," I said "the last time we even saw a steak was back in your home town at the Steak Loft almost six weeks ago."

This was enough for them. They scurried outside and opened up an immense deepfreeze. In moments they were back with a case of frozen T-bones.

"How many do you want?" Clint asked, meanwhile prying off steaks with a cleaver.

"Would you like some mushrooms?" — this from Barry. "I know we have some around here somewhere."

He disappeared into a storeroom. Soon he returned with a No. 10 tin of buttered mushrooms.

Amidst a rich flow of conversation we prepared a steakfry fit for visiting nobility. These men were lonesome, aching for contact with someone from Outside. We spent three hours in the best of talk with them, and were longing to stay for more, but it was August 5th, eleven days late on our overall schedule. The men urged us to stay the night, since they were the only people in a camp designed for 45 men. They had been there alone for two weeks as watchmen, awaiting the barges which were due in three days, for the camp was to be dismantled and moved. They had freezers and storehouses filled with food, 43 empty bunks, and a great loneliness.

We extended our visit as long as we could, but finally convinced them and ourselves that we had to leave.

The camp itself had many buildings, aluminum trailer type, on skids with boardwalks between. There were bunk houses, a washroom, storehouses, mess hall, radio shack, and recreation room. Around the site were generators, trucks, dismantled oil rigs, and I know not what all, ready to be placed on the barges and taken away. The men told us that winter was the best time for drilling because the freeze made things firm. They drilled under huge floodlights, not worrying about day and night; as long as there was no wind blowing, the work was not too bad or too cold. In summer there was too much slush and muck. Summer was best for moving camps — in fact, the only time, for freeze-up started on the river on the first of September and break-up continued through most of June.

We told the men, "Look for our friend, Duc Meyer. He's only a few days behind us."

But they were not cheered. "We'll be gone in a few days," they protested.

Still we could not stay.

When we did leave, our hosts pressed us to load ourselves down with supplies. Their perishables would have to be abandoned, they said. But we were able to convince them that although we were thoroughly avaricious we just did not have room. They settled for stuffing a cardboard carton with goodies. We all chattered away down the hill, across the planks, to the wharf, and into the boats. Oh, how we wanted to stay!

That night we dined on luncheon meats as well as our dried foods, and I thought wistfully of clean bunkbeds and a warm shower as I finished up the dinner dishes and straightened the kitchen before turning in.

I didn't do a very good job, because I broke one of my own rules: I forgot to put the lid on Orphan Annie, and that night Orphan Annie blew away and (presumably) drowned.

Anyone in the United States who grew up during the depression years must know what a Little Orphan Annie Shake-up Mug is. Back in the days before osterizers, when celluloid was virtually the only plastic known, every childish radio fan of Annie's drank at least one jar of Ovaltine so that an Orphan Annie Shake-up Mug could be sent for accompanied by the proper coupon and the proper amount of money. Somehow in our camping forays the plastic cannister we bring for mixing juices and powdered milk has come to be known as "Orphan Annie." This year our Annie was a plastic quart jar with a green top. The top had its own special use, being just the right size for a biscuit cutter. Having grown tired of chasing down the lid, I made a rule that the lid would always be placed on the jar, except when in use as a biscuit cutter. Then one night I left the jar in one place, the lid in another.

I heard the jar rattling around over the rocks during the night, but figured the wind was pushing it around a little and I'd just pick it up somewhere down the beach in the morning. The wind grew stronger, the jar landed in the river, the waves filled the jar, and Orphan Annie was gone forever. I kept the green lid to use for biscuits, and mixed the breakfast juice in a Teflon pot, but it just wasn't the same as being shaken up in a mug. But, as it turned out, we didn't have to mourn long.

My log for the day reads: "Beautiful day. What weather! Camped at a bend where Thunder River comes in on a shale beach between three-hundred-foot cliffs. Feasted on steaks from the oil crew."

We had been in so many strikingly beautiful campsites. It was hard to believe we had found another one still different from the rest. Along this wide river the height of the cliffs was stunning. Just behind us stood a tiny thatch-roofed log cabin, almost hidden by the tangle of bush. When we walked by it on the way to the cliff top it looked older than a hundred years, but I imagine it was inhabited as recently as the 1930's. Our view from the top beggared description and we scared ourselves looking down on our miniaturized camp.

That night we finished our next to last gin bottle, so with proper ceremony Devon and the boys buried it. They selected a big piece of shale, about two feet by two feet, and, using a marker pen I found in the bottom of my purse, they wrote a suitable epitaph. "Here lies a gin bottle, killed by the Nickersons on August 6, 1966. R.I.P." Then they spent the rest of the evening tossing humming rocks in the river with David-slings. This had been a growing pastime on quiet evenings. Devon had fashioned a sling from a bit of leather and a piece of nylon cord, and had become quite adept at choosing stones whose shape would make the most interesting sounds.

In the morning I passed by the little mound on the way to scoop up some water for our breakfast. I had a sudden inspiration. Quickly I exhumed the bottle, rinsed it thoroughly, and promoted it to Orphan Annie. The marker was returned to its natural state, and camp cookery resumed its normal tenor (if it is normal to have grade-school boys taking a perverse delight in mixing their morning fruit juice in a *real gin bottle!*).

Before we left that morning Devon and I paddled a few yards into the mouth of the Thunder River for a drink of fresh water, a face wash, and a teeth brush. In the clear stream Devon spotted some grayling. Brian and I left him happily fishing, and went on to join the others. As we came out of the mouth of the little river a baby seagull, hiding in the bushes nearby, panicked and leaped into the river, swimming ahead of us. The current of the Mackenzie picked him up and swept him downstream. We lost sight of him, although once in awhile the mother seagull would fly over and call to him. When we caught up to Nick and Linc, about a half mile downstream, there was the seagull up on the beach, walking back along the shore to Thunder River and Mother.

Our goal that day was the Travaillant River which we made easily. We spent part of the early evening fishing, and caught a large pike. I made an especially good batch of corn bread, and with pike and beef stew and fruit cocktail inside us we were sufficed. Coffee cups in hand, Nick and I were propped up beside the campfire when Devon called out,

"I see a boat upstream."

There, just above the horizon, we could see the first white speck of a boat. We waited to pick up the sound of the engines, but no sound came. We looked for the boat to grow larger, but its size did not increase fast enough.

We trained our field glasses on it, all three pairs, and Devon shouted, "It's a sail. It must be Duc!"

In wild excitement the younger boys dashed about the camp, shouting, "It's Duc, it's Duc! He's made it! He's made it!"

"You know," I remarked to Nick. "He's probably been worrying about us all summer, and listen to the boys. They've been worrying about him."

At a long-abandoned Hudson's Bay Trading Post the author relaxes in a battered rocking chair while son Devon slouches in the doorway. The cabin interior is a mess; only a desperate situation could have driven us to stay inside.

A wild ride up the steep clay cliffs on the pallet of a fork lift truck to the oil exploration camp near Little Chicago. Driver Clint Campbell and bare chested Barry Armstrong do not seem to mind the mosquitoes.

Devon, followed by Lincoln (in beaded moose jerkin given to him at Norman Wells) explores the living quarters of the oil camp. Bunk house units have single and double rooms with electric light and heat; laundry and washrooms have plenty of hot and cold running water. The food is top quality, served in great quantity in a comfortable mess hall. With good pay and no way to spend it, one might think oil exploration work would be oversubscribed, but no pay has yet been devised to cure loneliness.

Reunion. Facing the camera in his lightweight summer parka, Luther (Duc) Meyer smiles to see his friends who he last greeted almost 3800 miles ago.

"Do we have anything left of dinner?" asked Nick.

As it happened, we did, thanks to my lazy habit of not cleaning up dishes until I'm good and ready. The pike had added to our supplies, and there was a nice portion of that, too. I put on the coffee pot, warmed up the stew, put the pike nearby, opened the last can of oranges, and buttered a piece of corn bread. The boys and Devon pranced up the shore, shouting and waving. Nick dug out our last bottle of gin.

Soon the little kayak, its sloop rig billowing in the brisk breeze, came sailing into the mouth of the Travaillant River. Another moment and Luther Duc Meyer stepped ashore.

"The Nickersons, I presume?" he laughed.

"Duc! Duc! Duc!" Brian and Linc shouted, jumping up and down.

I hugged him so hard he winced. Nick and Dev pounded him on the back.

Then we all stood and grinned at each other. Nick handed him a mug of juice, saying,

"Come on into the kitchen. You're just in time for dinner."

16 «
THE DELTA

Luther (Duc) Meyer was 68 years old when he made his first trip by kayak, alone, the length of the Mackenzie River. He did not stop that time at Inuvik, as we intended to do, but continued another 56 miles through the delta, then 14 miles across an arm of the Beaufort Sea to the Eskimo town of Tuktoyaktuk on the edge of the Arctic Ocean. The following year he made almost the same journey in a motorboat taking for a companion his young grandson. In 1965 he was again alone, in a kayak. At Inuvik he had a Yukon scow built and bought an 18-horsepower kicker to take him back upriver. He left later in the season than he should have, and at the Ramparts he ran into bad weather and bad luck. He was swamped, but was able to return to Good Hope where he dried out in the jail, next to where we had camped, with Mr. and Mrs. Hayes' help. Here also he received treatment for his injuries (a cut head, a cracked rib) and flew home.

This year, at 71, Duc was back on his beloved Mackenzie, carrying a tiny sail rigged to his kayak. He traveled with his boat filled to the gunwales with paperback books which he distributed to villages and schools along the way. Being also a working reporter he carried a typewriter and a tape recorder too. This was the man who introduced us to the Northwest Territories, and gave us valuable information about the country and its people. At breakfast we made our plans.

"How are you folks planning to get out to Tuk?" he asked.

"Not paddling," was Nick's immediate reply.

"We hope we can catch a ride on a tugboat," I said.

"By the way," Devon asked. "Whatever happened to your scow?"

"I don't really know," Duc answered. "I think the barge took it down to Inuvik, but I don't know what shape it's in. And I don't know where the kicker is either."

We talked for awhile, and decided we would play it by ear when the time came. Then we went on to the question of where we would stay in Inuvik.

This was more of a problem than it might appear at first glance. Out in the bush there is no lack of clean campsites and pure water. But none of the towns along the way make a business-like provision for the camper. There are no designated parks, campsites, or areas where this kind of tourist can pay a fee and pitch a tent for a few nights and find pure water and sanitary facilities. You take your chances on the hospitality of the people—a hospitality that can always be found, but sometimes you wonder if you are imposing. At Inuvik we needed a two-week camp.

Duc had a couple of ideas, but was not ready to tell them yet. He assured us, "Don't worry. They will be glad to see you. Then we can decide together how to explore the delta."

At no time did we plan to kayak to Inuvik together. Our family considers 25 miles a good day's run, Duc averaged more like sixty. Now we were to say goodbye for about ten days.

Just before Duc's departure, Brian came running up to Devon with the news,

"A great big fish just jumped!"

"Where, show me!" said Dev, ever the fisherman. He grabbed up a pole and followed Brian.

Duc, who never fishes on these trips but exists, I am convinced, on soup, tea, and air, came along to look. On the second cast Devon hooked a two-foot pike. He played him well on the lightweight trout line. The fish performed by jumping from the water, plunging deep, sulking, then emerging in another series of jumps and plunges. But Devon's skill and luck were too much for the fish and he was landed.

For a few moments it looked as though Dev had almost won another convert to the fishing game, but I think the hanker in Duc's eye soon passed, and I doubt that he has yet rushed out to buy himself a line.

At parting Duc reminded us, "Look for me through Bob and Julie Woodland. I'll leave word with them where I'm staying."

With a few deft strokes of his paddle, he pointed his little kayak into the stream. Then he hoisted his sail, caught the wind which was still blowing from the south, waved jauntily, and was on his way.

An hour later we followed. Devon rigged a sail from a large piece of plastic and scarcely touched a paddle all day. We made an easy 25 miles. It was another wonderful day, and we enjoyed it to the utmost, lazy and relaxed in the extreme, letting the wind and current do the work. We did not know it then, of course, but it was our last such easy day.

It took us four more days to cover the remaining fifty miles to the village of Arctic Red River. A storm kept us from moving for one 24-hour period and contrary winds made us earn every mile. Ten miles from Arctic Red we made one of the prettiest camps ever, on a beach of white sand in a sheltered cove where another crystal creek sparkled into the Mackenzie. But when we broke camp it took us almost four hours to toil those ten miles. We were ready to spend the night in town at the drop of an invitation.

The landing dock area of the town is in the Arctic Red River mouth. There is room for a floatplane to land and take off, and a floating wharf for it to discharge and take on passengers or cargo. A boat entering this harbor area skirts native fishnets anchored well out into the stream. The dock itself is made up of floating logs about the size of telephone poles only casually joined together and tied to shore, making it a real feat to climb ashore successfully.

At the top of the road from the dock stands the Roman Catholic church and the top of the next hill has the Hudson's Bay post. The top of the third hill has the Royal Canadian Mounted Police station. Our first call was the Bay.

Again our spirits rose at the sight of a stack of mail from home. We bought more coffee, tried for bacon (which, of course, was "fresh out"), and ate a couple of candy bars apiece right there in the store.

From the Bay we crossed over to the R.C.M.P. Here we learned that even though Duc had checked in a few days before and told them we were behind schedule, the men were planning to start preliminary searching for us had we not arrived this day. We were impressed by their concern, and they were sincerely relieved to see us.

By now we were rested and ready to be off even though the wind still was against us. We walked back to the beach, and were about to disembark when the local priest, Father Colas, came down the hill. To him we owe our thanks for advising us to cross the river immediately rather than attempt it further downstream, wind and waves being more hazardous there than here. This was information that only someone resident to the area could know, and we followed his advice to the letter.

A full two hours later we made one of the more unusual camps of our trip: we were about two hundred yards downstream from an Indian fish camp.

Father Colas had told us about the place. He said, "There is a family named Williams. They are good people. They will be happy to have you nearby, and there is a son about the age of your young sons."

We got a good look at the camp as we paddled by. There was one large tent, a pole framework for a second, and a fish rack, partly filled with drying whitefish. Two large scows with kickers were tied at the river's edge, and a canoe stood on shore. Eight sled dogs were staked out at one end of camp and two at the other. A boy of about ten years was playing with the larger group of dogs. Two women sat at an outdoor table cleaning fish. A man stood near them, watching as we passed, then went up the beach to tend his nets.

As I fixed dinner, Brian and Linc walked up to the camp to see if they could meet the boy, but the moment he saw them approach he darted into the tent and would not come out. The boys, although sorry to be so feared, were intrigued by the fish-cleaning process so turned their attention to Mrs. Williams and her friend who were busy at work.

At last the Indian boy, Charles, overcame his shyness and emerged from the tent. The three boys were soon playing simple, non-equipment games — one favorite was to toss a large stick in the current, then stone it as it rode by. The drift of the game eventually brought the boys down to our camp, and we followed back upstream to meet the adults. Now that the children had broken the ice, it was not hard to get a conversation started. About 10:30 we went back to our camp and settled down for the night, but before sleep came a boatload of friends drove in to visit the Williams family. We think they dined at midnight on fresh fillets of whitefish — somehow it seemed like an even more stylish hour than dinner at eight.

In the morning the Williams family visited our camp, and we shared coffee all around. Mr. Williams and Nick talked about fishing and hunting. They fired a few rounds from the guns, squinted wisely through the field glasses, inspected the kayaks, discussed the weather. Mrs. Williams, who spoke no English, but understood the language, asked questions through her friend Clara, who had been to missionary school. We talked of cooking, looked at the camp oven, examined the tent, discussed the warmth of down sleeping bags. We might well have been camping in a park at home in the States, comparing notes with the family camped next dooor.

We took to our boats late that day. Our goal was to pass Point Separation, the entrance to the Mackenzie Delta, and from now on we would be more than ever dependent on our ability to read our maps.

That night's camp, on August 13th, summer ended and fall began, an autumn that was to last only two and a half weeks. During the day we had passed stands of trees, spruce, alder, birch, and willow, wherein we noted yellow leaves. We wondered if it might not be some kind of disease. "Mid-August is too early for fall colors," we said. But that same night the temperature dropped to the twenties. In the morning frost covered the ground and a half-inch of ice stood in the water bucket!

On this day we had only seventy miles to go to Inuvik. After eight miles we made our first sharp turn to the east and entered the narrow, twisting channel that would take us to the town. From this point we had very little current to help us. At the same time we were on a waterway whose width was no longer measured in miles but in yards so that wind and storm ceased to be problems. Now it was pull, pull, pull, for sixty-two miles, but we had been seven weeks on the river and we were in physical condition to tackle the job.

Our first East Channel camp found us cooking dinner early when a motorboat with three men came by. They turned in to visit for awhile, and we of course served coffee. These men were part Indian, called "Metis" in the North. As the boat grounded, Nick called out "Toss me your line," and on catching it pulled the boat partly up on shore.

The driver stepped out remarking, "You know, I've pulled in many a white man's boat, but this is the first time a white man has ever pulled up mine."

"Well," said Nick, "it's about time one of us did. My name's Nickerson," and the introductions went around with the coffee cups.

We talked for almost half an hour. Unlike the men of Jean Marie and other villages, these included me in their conversation. Apparently their heritage and their association with the modern world allowed women to enlarge their social world. I asked about Duc Meyers.

"Oh, the man who came down alone in a kayak? He is in town. We think he is at the R. C. Hostel."

This was the local terminology for the school dormitory run by the Oblate Fathers. The other dormitory is Church of England. We doubted that these places were taking in roomers, but at least we knew Duc was safe.

"What about the five young men who came in the canoes?" Devon asked.

"You mean the Beatles? Two are working for me. Another one is a mechanic in a garage. One is still looking for a job, and one flew home. They are good boys."

Our coffee and visit ended. The men climbed in their boat and roared on their way to Arctic Red River.

Three more days of river life remained to us. The water was siltier than ever, the current more and more sluggish as channel after channel broke off and the delta spread its web. It is hard

to give exact dimensions of this region, but the distance from
Point Separation to the ocean is over one hundred and fifty
miles by river; and the distance from Inuvik to Aklavik, crossing the width of the delta at its mid-point by following a maze
of channels, is around eighty river miles. We paddled seventeen
miles that day, and were now beginning to hear noises related
to civilization. Once in a while the sound of a chain saw would
ring out across the channels. Several planes flew over during
the day, indicating a landing strip or port not many air miles
ahead. Almost every promising bend in the channel carried a
chain of red plastic motorboat oil bottles, now serving as floats
to keep nets in place for the commercial fishing industry of the
delta.

In the early afternoon we came to a spot in the river where
a large outcropping of rock formed a scenic spot for a cabin.
The place was known as Fabian's and the men we had met
mentioned that there was also a fish camp nearby and suggested we stop to visit. Here we were cordially greeted by Mrs.
Rachel Reindeer and her two children, Esther and Wayne. The
four young people were soon acquainted and eagerly swapping
comic books. Mrs. Reindeer had just finished cooking two pans
of delicious-smelling bannock, and invited us in for tea.

"You are just in time for the messages," she said. "I always
listen to the messages."

Now we had no idea what in the world "the messages"
might be, but as soon as Mrs. Reindeer reached over and
switched on her table model transistor radio we thought we
knew: some kind of inspirational program, no doubt. To our
surprise we were introduced to a way of life in the delta. "Messages" refers, no more, no less, to news, instructions, greetings,
directions, appeals — messages — sent from one private party
to another, or from people to people, through the courtesy of
the delta's one and only radio station, CHAK. These are sent
free, at one in the afternoon, and repeated at 6:30 at night.
They are preceded by "announcements" which are generally
commercial in nature, and by "news" and followed by local
weather reports. Before we left Inuvik we had cause to use
"messages" twice. Without this method of communication life

Devon, chef of the moment, barbecues a pike on a turning spit powered by two flashlight batteries. This barbecue, known as a Flash-o-barb, will turn an eight-pound roast with ease. Two batteries give over twenty hours of work.

The town of Arctic Red River guards the beginning of the Mackenzie Delta. From here the land is flat, the tundra starts soon after, and the river branches into a maze of channels. The Red River mouth lies out of this picture just to the left, beyond the point of land on which stands the Roman Catholic Church.

After making a frantic swim across the channel directly in front of our kayaks, this bear stood and regarded us, panting, before turning away and grumbling off into the underbrush. We were less than five miles from Inuvik.

Lincoln (left) and Brian hold a dried reindeer hide at Reindeer Depot. The log cabin and the modern buildings in the background contrast sharply, but both are used by the Eskimo reindeer herders; some for storage, and some for dwellings. There is electricity, but no indoor plumbing.

Bear tracks!

would be quite different for the people of the delta. In a few short years it has become something of an institution.

Today we heard a message in which the parents of four children were asked to pick them up at the Inuvik Hospital at 3:00 p.m. when they were to be released. "Please remember to bring their shoes." Another was a request from a little Eskimo girl to her grandfather at Tuktoyaktuk to send more muktuk on the "sked" (scheduled air line). There was a handful of birthday greetings. One man sent word to his family that he had missed the plane out of Old Crow and would be home on the next "sked." There were many more.

We listened, fascinated, to the glimpses of life revealed by these homely messages.

Mrs. Reindeer told us, "Maybe there is one for you."

"Who would send to us?" I asked.

"That Mr. Meyer, maybe, or the Beatles. They said you are coming."

"Did they stop here?" asked Devon.

"Oh yes," said our friend. "They were awful tired and pretty sick. They camp here, then get a tow to Inuvik."

We listened while Mrs. Reindeer told us of our Norman Wells friends, who, nearly out of food and existing almost entirely on flour, beans and fish, had fought those big cargo canoes through the delta to her camp and asked permission to stay and rest for a day on her beach. She sensed their weakened condition and fed them tea, bannock, and a hearty stew. Then her husband, a carpenter at Inuvik who was visiting home for the next day, towed them to town with his motorboat.

"Mr. Meyer, he almost camp here too," she said.

Duc had pulled in, asked permission to camp, and just started to unpack when a motorboat "came for him." We thought about that for a while, and decided that he must have been given a chance to hitch a tow with a passing fisherman and changed his mind about staying. Only later did we find out that Bob and Julie Woodland, deciding it was about time for Duc to show up, had bundled themselves and their three children into Bob's speedboat one evening after work and come up the channel searching for him.

After our visit we made our thanks to our hostess and waited for our younger boys to say their goodbyes. It was the only time we were invited inside a native's fish camp tent, and we were well pleased with what we saw. The floor was the ground, strewn with fragrant dried grass and partly covered with throw rugs. Just inside the entrance stood a tiny cast-iron wood stove. A large stovepipe stuck a good three feet out in front of the tent, horizontally, so that sparks would not go in the direction of the canvas. A raised wooden platform, about three feet wide at the sides and deeper across the back, ran in a U-formation along the walls of the tent. To the left as you entered, this platform held dishes and cooking equipment neatly arranged on shelves made of crates. The rest of the platform was covered with throw rugs and hides, making a comfortable lounging pavilion by day and sleeping room at night. The place was airy, clean, attractive, casual, and altogether livable. As I glanced at Mrs. Reindeer's modern radio, and at the glasses she was wearing, and thought of Mr. Reindeer's boat and kicker, I thought again of how possible it is to live with the comforts of the modern world while still enjoying much of the simplicity of the old ways.

No clear stream could we find for our last camp. However, we came upon a huge wide bend in the channel, with an inviting beach, and went ashore. It was not long before the boys discovered ripe blueberries: tons of them. Even before dinner was ready they were back in camp with a potful.

Meanwhile two native fishermen came in sight, in an open motorboat, and pulled up to a large net strung into the river just above our camp. We waved at them as they worked, and the boys ran over to see what they were doing. Soon the boys were back, and the two fishermen went on their way, but they left part of their equipment on the beach.

"They're going to camp here too," Linc reported.

"Good," said Nick. "Get out the coffee pot."

Now that was silly because the coffee pot was always first unpacked and last to go, but I knew what he meant. There are very few gestures of hospitality you can make when living on carefully-rationed dehydrated food, but an extra couple of pounds of coffee in the rations can open the floodgates of communication. So later, when the men returned and set up their camp we had them over for a klatch. They were shy at first, but the younger boys were so disarming with their questions about netting fish and their excitement over the art of setting proper nets that the ice melted at last.

"See," said one of the men, "there's a fish now."

We looked out at the net floats where he was pointing, and saw two or three bobbing up and down. Something was struggling under the water — a fish, of course.

"Pike are no good. They fight, and break the nets."

Judging from the fights we'd had in angling for them we could see their point. We told them about the pike we had caught a few days back.

"When we opened him up he had two birds in his gullet — you'd think he'd be too stuffed to snap at a lure."

"No," said the men, "they are pigs, and no good eating. No good when you have whitefish anyhow."

We said we had never caught any whitefish, and they went on to explain, "They not bite on hooks. You catch them with nets."

They went back to their camp for dinner, but soon one of them returned with a large, cleaned whitefish.

We ate our whitefish for breakfast, throwing it directly on the wire griddle that formed our stove. We had fresh blueberry pancakes to accompany this delicacy, which made a superlative breakfast.

Wisps of fog rose from the river as we launched for the last fifteen miles of our total thousand. Only a few minutes on our way we thought we heard our first sounds of town.

"Quiet and listen," we told each other and strained our ears. Sure enough, we could hear auto horns, a generator, the noise of trucks in low gear. From a distance of seven and a half air miles, fifteen river miles, the town of Inuvik makes itself heard. We had forgotten to think about it the night before, but that had been our last sleep in the quiet and serenity of a bush camp.

The day wore on. We had to work hard, but we were so filled with anticipation over reaching our goal that this day we never seemed to tire.

Only an hour before town, as we moved down a large straightaway, Devon heard a noise ahead of him and to his right and called back to us:

"Look there!"

On the bank, about two hundred yards ahead, stood a black bear, poised to enter the river. We thought he would turn and run, but to our astonishment he elected to swim directly across in front of us. Immediately we went after him.

To my intense annoyance I found I had only eight feet of film in my camera. It takes forever to load my ancient model, so I put the camera down and joined the chase. Soon we were within ten yards of the bear, and maintaining this discreet distance we gabbled at him as he wheezed and puffed and puffed and struggled to get away from us. Nick clicked off 35-mm. pictures as the animal reached shore and clambered wearily out on the bank. There he stood, panting and staring at us, too exhausted to growl or even run away. At last he caught his breath and waddled off.

"A fitting welcome to Inuvik," Nick commented.

"Do you suppose we should thank the local Chamber of Commerce?" asked Dev.

"Boy, that's better than the Jungle Ride at Disneyland," said Linc and Brian.

"I sure hope you got some good pictures," I grumbled. "Next trip I'm adding a five-hundred-foot magazine to this camera!"

We toiled on. A slight, but meaningful headwind met us as we made our last turn into the two-mile stretch before Inuvik, "just to keep us honest," we decided. The town sparkled before us in the late afternoon sunshine.

Slowly, slowly buildings took on shape and identity. Sounds merged into the hum of a living town. Excitement grew in us with every pull of the paddles.

And then we were there.

17 «

INUVIK

Brian and Lincoln scampered up the shore. Devon stood and stargazed across the water. Nick turned to me, held out his arms, and I walked into the warmest bear-hug in the world.

"We did it!" he kept saying. "We did it, we did it!"

"But of course," I answered, and kissed my husband as a conquering hero should be kissed.

Hand in hand we wandered up the road into town, gawking at the newness of this village which had only been dedicated in 1961. We passed several people on the way who smiled and said "hello." When a car pulled up alongside of us, carrying two preschoolers and a baby in a car seat, I thought it was just a mother letting a curious kindergartener have a better look at a bunch of strangers.

But when the lady leaned over across her children and called, "Hello, Nickersons. I'm Julie Woodland. We've been looking for you!" I knew we were no longer strangers in town.

Julie drove us to her home where we greeted Duc, well settled in the spare bedroom. Soon Bob Woodland came home. They told us then that the next night they had planned to come upriver to search for us and we had a good laugh over the thought of their speedboat towing three kayaks in a row.

"We found Duc last week at Fabian's, you know," said Bob.

"I was ready to be found," Duc admitted.

We were able to get two rooms at the Mackenzie Hotel, one with bath, and one without, for a special family rate of $32.00. These rooms would only be available for three nights because a group of government VIP's was due Saturday and from then on the place was booked. Although we did not say so, this news did not exactly shatter us. We could well afford thirty-two dollars worth of warm baths and a good night's sleep, but we had no intention of spending four hundred and sixteen dollars more just for twelve more days of beds and a roof over our heads. I got the first confirmation of my resolve to move out soon when, on taking my turn for that long-awaited bath, I found that all the hot water had been used by the two boys and the two men. So once more I used the quick dip method of bathing instead of that nice, long, steamy soak I had been anticipating.

That evening we wandered about the town. Duc and the Woodlands were going to a surprise anniversary party given in honor of Slim and Agnes Semmler, the free traders in town, and we were at liberty to get our first impressions.

In the town square there is a monument dedicated to Inuvik, which in Eskimo means "the place of man." The design is an open, three-part sphere, symbolic of the three races in the town's population: Indian, Eskimo, and White. Engraved below are these words:

"This was the first community north of the Arctic Circle built to provide the normal facilities of a Canadian town. It was designed not only as a base for development and administration but as a centre to bring education, medical care, and new opportunity to the people of the Western Arctic. [Dated] 21 June 1961."

In other words, Inuvik is an experiment in social welfare: a living thesis which states that through education and opportunity a simple culture can enter the twentieth century culture, take the best of the new, keep the best of the old, and eventually become self-supporting.

This is a colorful town, literally as well as figuratively. The houses and most of the business and government buildings are a symphony in pastels: pale pink, fragile yellow, powder blue, off-white, sea-foam green, mauve, chartreuse, turquoise, peach. The boldest colors are, perhaps, the occasional bone-white trim, a milk-chocolate brown, and a restrained shrimp. The overall effect, at least in my opinion, is charming. Also, it is very practical in locating specific houses since they are totally standardized in construction, and the numbering system "grew like Topsy."

We walked on wide board sidewalks which edge oil and gravel streets. Macadam roads and concrete walks probably could not survive the extremes of temperature and the quirks of building on permafrost. We passed by the large government school, formally named "Sir Alexander Mackenzie" and known everywhere as SAM. For awhile we watched a well-played softball game, one of a summer recreation program, a round-robin tournament involving at least eight teams. There were several leagues in different age groups and for boys, girls, men, and women. This game happened to be played by young women of high school and college age, and the stands were filled with interested spectators.

Later we walked by the local movie house which shows five different films per week, all recent releases from the States. Next to the theater was a cafe-soda fountain with a juke box and in an adjacent room were pool and billiard tables. We noticed a large community curling rink, and there were signs posted around the town advertising a Bingo Night at the social hall of the Roman Catholic church. Many bicycles were on the streets and not a few motor scooters and lightweight motor-cycles. By now we also knew that Inuvik was a hunters', fishers', and campers' paradise. Adventurous people went water skiing in the summer. Swimming was available too, albeit not in an indoor, heated pool. And what a spot for winter sports! The school had a good gymnasium and a small but growing public library. Among the clubs are Lions, Girl Guides, Boy Scouts, Canadian Women's Institute, and various church and school-sponsored fellowships. The town was still in a building boom with unlimited opportunity for people to get into business, particularly service business, regardless of age, if willing to work consistently.

But it wasn't long before we were to hear that the young people complained of having nothing to do; the parents remarked that the schools were this, that, and the other thing, but never any good; and the elderly felt that the medical service was just one long "hurry up and wait." Prices were too high everywhere, everyone drank too much, the youth were forgetting, ignoring, flaunting the old ways, therefore delinquency was rising. The government was interfering too much with the town's development. The government was not doing enough to help the town grow. They even had a litter problem!

As Bob Hope's book titles it, "We Never Left Home."

Of course we didn't get all this during that first night's stroll but even when we did learn more and more about the settlement's growing pains, it could not dampen our enthusiasm for the town. We know Inuvik has everything needed for a full, rich, productive life: it just hasn't grown to believe it yet.

At last we stopped our wanderings and went to our rooms, anticipating a good night's sleep between fresh white sheets on a comfortable bed, the first since the Macdonald Hotel eight weeks ago. As we entered our room we were met by a blast of warm air.

"Do you suppose there's a fire?" I asked.

"Can't be. No smoke," said Nick.

"Maybe the heater has been on."

It had been and it was yet. Centrally controlled, the thing was putting out B.T.U.'s by the jillion.

"Too bad they couldn't direct some of that to their hot-water tank," I grumbled.

"Up with the windows," Nick answered cheerfully, and with a bit of a struggle got one sash raised a full six inches.

That nice, freshly-made bed was waiting though, so we tossed off all the blankets and climbed in. No sooner had our heads touched the pillows than a tremendous sound erupted from the room directly below.

"Oh no!" I moaned.

"I had forgotten how well I can live without that," said Nick.

The noise was the beginning of three hours of loud, wild USA rock, plus all the rest of the noises that go with a pub full of people. We knew that the Mackenzie Hotel had two bars: the Mackenzie Lounge and the Aurora Lounge. We were right over the latter, commonly known around the town as the Zoo.

We actually considered going down and joining them—not in a spirit of fun, but only because it was impossible to sleep; but we were honestly so tired that we settled for dozing until the closing hour. Then ensued the almost fascinating problem of the partying patrons navigating the steps down from the hotel porch to the sidewalk. We never did get up and look out the window, but I am sure that at least two people were so pleased with themselves for having made it down the six or seven steps safely that they climbed up and down them several times more, bragging and laughing, just to show themselves and their cheering friends that they could do it.

Inuvik goes to bed late and gets up early, at least in summer, so we were able to sleep in only until 6:30.

"Let's eat and check out," were Nick's earliest repeatable words.

At breakfast, in the little cafe around the corner, we discussed a place to camp.

"Maybe near where the Beatles have their tent," I suggested. We had spotted their camp the night before. (They were all working in town, their curly locks trimmed, their beards shaven, storing up funds for the time when they could resume their vagabonding.)

"Sounds fine," my husband agreed. "Maybe Duc and Bob can help us move."

We finished our breakfast in revived spirits, and walked down to Woodlands' with our plans made. (A stop by the hotel found Devon and the boys somehow still sleeping. Later when we complained to them about the noise they asked, "What noise?" and that took care of us.)

At the Woodlands' Julie greeted us warmly and announced, "Breakfast is ready."

"But, but, but . . ." we started.

Then we stopped and enjoyed a second meal.

We didn't have to camp after all, for that day Bob found us a place to stay. We moved to the two spare bedrooms of Fritz and Emma Feichtinger, unrolled our faithful sleeping bags, and for the next thirteen days were members of their family. This was not a business arrangement: Fritz would not hear of it. We were his guests. Needless to say, there are no adequate thanks for such hospitality.

Thursday, in addition to moving day, was a day of wandering free. Devon, who is a member of the Arctic Research Institute, was eager to get acquainted with the Inuvik Research Laboratory. The boys wanted to find the playground, check the local movie setup, and make some friends. Nick and I had first to make a visit to the bank and then to the Rehabilitation Centre, a store featuring native crafts almost directly across the street. Devon learned we had arrived too late in the week for him to be included on a trip to Herschel Island and Sachs Harbour, but he met some interesting people and found the spot where he was to spend his idle hours during our stay. One of the scientists was Dr. John Lobart, from Columbia University, a psychiatrist who was doing another summer of research in the Far North. His study concerned the emotional-psychological-sociological adjustments of the Eskimo to modern-day living. His wife and son had only recently arrived from the States to share his last three weeks in Inuvik. Dev was delighted to learn that Andre, the son, was almost 18, and even more delighted to find Andre an intelligent, interesting, articulate young man. He smoked a pipe, played guitar, was bilingual, and his second language, French, was Devon's second language too.

Nick and I found wonderful treasures in native furs and native crafts in the Rehab Centre. There were dress parkas of muskrat trimmed in wolverine, shipped across the delta from Aklavik for sale at the Inuvik Centre. There were working parkas of duffel with grenfel covers, made by the women right there in the shop. There were jackets of duffel trimmed in stroud, beaded and stroud-trimmed mukluks, pillows and wall hangings of many kinds of furs, authentic Eskimo dolls and miniature artifacts. The building was new, still under construction, designed to provide working room for the craftsmen and display and sale room for their products. The manager, Miss Naomi Griffin, answered our eager questions, introduced us to the half-dozen native women who were working, and sold us three parkas, a pillow, and an Eskimo doll.

The idea behind the Rehab, which is run as a cooperative, is, again, to help the native find his way in the modern world, in this case by learning to exploit his special talents and crafts. In creating dress parkas for Outside, at Aklavik, they are being taught to match pelts for beauty as well as grade pelts for quality. This is a real departure from the old ways of simply stitching together a random selection of muskrat skins for warmth. In Inuvik the parkas are of duffel, a material which looks like felt but which is of the same quality as the traditional Hudson's Bay Blanket. Grenfel is the name of an extremely close-woven cotton, and is used to cover the white duffel for beauty and cleanliness. The special flavor of Eskimo design and trim remains and is encouraged. I believe the authentic Eskimo duffel working parka and the fur dress parka for Outside combine the two essentials for quality styling: beauty and practicality.

The people in the rehab centres and fur cooperatives have many problems to solve. For one, native tanning is totally unsuitable for fur garments and trim other than those worn in the bush. Pelts must be exported, even as far away as St. Louis, Missouri, tanned, and re-imported to Canada. There are no commercial tanneries in the Northwest Territories. No one we talked to in the States or in southern Canada could say with any degree of accuracy what we would find in the way of furs and handcrafts on our journey, or give us a realistic estimate of their cost. At the Bay in Edmonton, in the sportswear department we found nylon jackets such as we would shop for in our favorite store back home. In the fur department we saw stoles, capes, and coats with all the distinctive styling of downtown, USA. The clerks thought we might find "something" further north, but they didn't know what and they didn't know where. Only when we reached Fort Simpson did we get some reliable-sounding information.

"Yes," said Sister Lemire, "you will find fur *parkys* north, but far north, in the delta, at the co-ops." Being in touch with her sister Grey Nuns, some of whom are stationed in Inuvik, she was also in touch with the times.

Although the native craftsman lacks in communication, advertising, and marketing his product, the work habits of the natives themselves constitute the big problem. We never expected to encounter the Land of Mañana 125 miles north of the Arctic Circle, but it is there: Work if necessary, until money is in the hand, then quit until the money is gone.

Still another problem involves authenticity of design and adulteration of quality. Since the White Man is so powerful, why not copy his designs? If the tourist will buy without examining carefully, why not substitute, for example, pieces made of wood instead of bone?

In the co-ops the jobs of the director include finding solutions to all these problems.

As we were talking to Miss Griffin, a little Eskimo lady entered, one quite grandmotherly in age and demeanor. She walked over to where two other Eskimo women were working, and took a chair beside them. They chatted away in Innuit. On her lap she had a plain brown paper bag.

Miss Griffin noticed the bag, but made no comment, allowing her to take her time. After about ten minutes, the little grandmother reached into the bag and pulled out a doll. Miss Griffin took her cue.

"And what's this?" she said, walking over to stand beside the chair.

The lady giggled, and looked away shyly. Miss Griffin held out her hand and the Eskimo lady gave her the doll.

"Hmm, hmmm," said Miss Griffin.

More giggles.

She brought the doll to us. It was an authentic piece of work, insofar as we could tell: the figure of a woman clad in muskrat fur parka, a thong tied about the waist, wearing leggings and gloves. The face was of soft hide, like chamois, with the features drawn in. I fell for it instantly, thinking what a perfect gift it would make from Devon to his girl.

But after we admired it, Miss Griffin went back to the artist and asked, "What's this?"

Up to now the Eskimo lady had been all smiles. Also she spoke only Innuit, so we doubted whether she could understand much of what was being said. We couldn't have been more mistaken. On this question her smile faded. Miss Griffin was pointing to the ruff around the parka hood.

"Where did you get this?" she asked. "Your blouse? An old scarf?"

Now we noticed that the ruff was made of some kind of piled fabric, like cheap black velvet, instead of fur as it should have been.

The lady looked away, a total picture of "No comprendo."

Miss Griffin continued, "Tablecloth? Curtains? Your glove?"

Many giggles! Quickly, but unsuccessfully, the lady hid her smiles behind the sleeve of her gingham Mother Hubbard.

Her questioner laughed too. "Your glove!" she repeated. "You know that's not so good."

Nods from the lady.

"You know it's not as much money."

A little frown—then a smile. More nods.

Miss Griffin then looked hard at the little doll and scowled slightly again. Seeming to reach some kind of conclusion she undid the little leather thong encircling the doll's waist. Then she shook the doll vigorously and brushed the fur carefully with a tiny nail brush. Running her finger over the offending parka, she "tch-tched" a little, then smiled at the Eskimo and named the price.

The little lady nodded vigorously and smiled too.

This was the doll we, or rather Devon, bought. Interestingly enough, he found no fault with the ruff, and thought the doll looked better with the sash. (If the tourist doesn't care about authenticity, why should the craftsman?)

From the Rehab, we found our way to Grolier Hall, the hostel run by the Oblate Fathers which during this week was hosting the first territorial convention of the Northern Canada Women's Institutes. This was a gathering of women from all over the Mackenzie and the North for the purpose of exchanging ideas and information relating to food, clothing, recreation, gardening, health, and general living in the North. Their program included lecture-demonstrations in cooking, gardening, handcrafts; there were speeches, banquets, field trips. All the northern races were represented, the delegates housed in the dormitory and sharing meals in the school dining hall.

Each delegation also brought prize examples of local handcrafts to be shown in a large exhibit, open to the public. Many of these items were for sale, so we bought a beautiful pair of women's mukluks with a design in sparkling blue and green beadwork, trimmed in unsheared beaver. We also bought a pair of crow boots to take home for a gift.

We met many of the delegates, even though the convention was ending. I remember talking to Mrs. Ida Aleekuk of Reindeer Station, and asking her if it had been a good convention.

She said, "Oh yes. Very nice. So many people and all so friendly."

Then she added, "You know, this is the first time I am at a convention. And this is the first time I live in the same house with white people."

I was so pleased at her openness, I asked a bold question, "Do you like us?"

She stopped a moment, seeming just a little startled by this directness, but then she said very seriously, "Yes, I like."

"Well," I said, "I have just come to Inuvik as a tourist, and this is the first time I have ever lived in the same house with an Eskimo."

Mrs. Aleekuk looked at me for a moment, her expression thoughtful. Then her eyes sparkled and her face lighted up.

"You like us?" she shot back.

"Yes, I like!"

We burst into laughter, joined by other women who were standing by listening. When we said goodbye, Mrs. Aleekuk knew that our family planned to visit Reindeer Station soon, and that we would meet again.

The reference to living with an Eskimo was no idle conversational gambit. Our hostess, Mrs. Emma Feichtinger, was Eskimo. Attractive, intelligent, shy, and scared of these overwhelming American tourists, Emma took us into her home because her other white friends and her husband said it was the thing to do. By the end of our stay, we were her friends too.

Later that day Devon introduced us to Dr. Lobart while we were having an afternoon snack at the cafe. Soon he invited us to a cocktail party at his home on Saturday night, and we accepted at once.

Dinner that Thursday night was at the Woodlands': a great feast of genuine Italian spaghetti that Julie had been brewing all day. Bob was brimming with the news that a local commercial fisherman would be happy to take us with him on his boat as he went to various fish camps "throughout the entire delta." He was going to call in the morning before leaving, and we should be ready at the Woodlands' if interested. Julie also reported that she had to work at the community Bingo Friday night and invited us all to come along. Our social calendar was filling. We still had not discovered how we were to get out to Tuk, but no one seemed to think it much of a problem. There were always places in chartered planes, or in a boat or even as a last resort on the sked. These things "occur as they occur," so we let it pass.

Next day, however, we missed connections with our boat. We waited at Bob's, but no phone call came. We learned later that our fisherman had forgotten his offer and left without us. When he did remember, he figured that we could come with him next time, early next week. But late that day his new kicker "froze up" and he was without his big boat and kicker for the next ten days. We felt again a little of that mañana spirit.

During the day the tug *Ooqallupik*, but of course generally called *Ook-pik*, arrived at Inuvik. The skipper was Mr. Hill, and we managed to locate him by phone. This was the same Northern Affairs tug which had tooted seven times at us back up the river.

"We understand you are allowed to carry passengers. Are you going out to Tuk?" we asked.

"Yes," he answered, "there are some teachers returning from their holiday Outside and we will be carrying their baggage Tuesday."

The whole family was thrilled at the thought of riding a tug out through the delta to the ocean. This was the mode of transportation we had dreamed of as an ideal conclusion to our river wanderings because the tugs and barges had been so much a part of our eight weeks' paddling.

Mr. Hill remembered saluting us on the beach.

"We wanted to come over and visit with you, but we thought it too shallow. So we anchored for the night about a half-mile upstream."

So that was why the motor sound had suddenly stopped! We assured him it had indeed been shallow and parted with arrangements to meet the next day, Saturday, to sign some necessary "release of liability" papers. The passage was free but an insurance formality had to be met.

That night we went to the bingo game, confident that we were at last on our way to Tuk. We wondered if we would have two or three days there, or just overnight and a few hours. Soon, however, we were caught up in the fun of people watching at a Community Bingo.

Bingo is a disease endemic to North America; of this I am convinced. Highly contagious and relatively harmless, it is all the same whether caught at a charity social or in a Nevada gambling house. I have played bingo where the room was filled with a majority of Caucasions and a sprinkling of Orientals and Negroes. This night there was a majority of Eskimos and a sprinkling of Indians and whites. Nick sat in a corner with his sketch pad, looking every inch the artist with his neatly-trimmed beard and his quick-moving pencil. Julie was treasurer and presided over the money at the end of the room, but I was one of four change makers and card sellers, so could wander everywhere. The only thing different about the game was that even the children could play, if accompanied by their parents. Brian and Linc thought it grand, although they never won a thing.

The next morning Nick called Mr. Hill from the Woodlands' to make an appointment for signing papers. I didn't pay attention to the call, but when Nick turned away from the phone I could see something was wrong.

"What's up?" I asked.

"We're out of luck, there's been a change of plans."

"Oh, no. What now?"

"Well," said Nick, "the tug is going first to Arctic Red River and back. Then a week from Tuesday it's going out to Tuk. We're still welcome to come along."

Lincoln stands by a cut-away section of one of Inuvik's main utilidors. The top pipe carries super heated water under high pressure. The bottom pipes carry cold water and sewage. Constant circulation is necessary to prevent freezing in the Arctic winter.

A stile over a utilidor. The homes are raised on piles two feet above the ground to keep the permafrost from melting and causing the buildings to sink. The utilidors enter the houses in a four-foot crawl space and the porches enter above this space at "ground floor" level.

Inuvik, the modern village in the Eastern Mackenzie Delta, as viewed from a bush plane. The trees in the foreground, mostly spruce, grow to an average height of about 10 feet.

The Roman Catholic Church at Inuvik. Built by the Oblates of Mary Immaculate under the guidance of Father Adam, it is known as the Igloo Church. The buildings in the right background form one of the two hostels for boarding students.

There wasn't really much of anything to say. We had no yen for a round trip to Arctic Red again. And a week from Tuesday was the day our plane left for home.

"You know," Nick murmured, "it's like trying to pick up quicksilver."

"Three days down, and ten to go, and we're still without a plan," was Devon's comment.

At this point, Duc came to the rescue.

"You know, people, you can always use my scow."

"I thought it was being remodeled," Nick said.

"Well, no, they haven't gotten around to it yet. It's still up on the beach but it has a foot of mud in the bottom. I can have it cleaned out for you.

Nick and Dev looked at each other. "We'll do it! May we? Is it all right?"

Their enthusiasm was contagious. In just a few minutes plans and ideas were zipping back and forth, which all resolved at last into: Clean up the boat today, install Bob's 28-horse-power kicker (instead of Duc's 18) this afternoon, and assemble gas cans and fuel this evening. The Woodlands, Duc, and the Nickersons would take the scow, and Feichtingers their own speedboat, and we would caravan down to Reindeer Station tomorrow. This would serve as a practice trip before going out to Tuk. We would take a picnic lunch, and put a pot roast on slow simmer for our return. Happily the two men took buckets, brushes, and rags down to the beach. In a little more than three hours they had the scow mucked out, scrubbed down, and ready to launch.

Dinner was with the Woodlands again who made it clear that we were their guests every night for our entire stay. Then Devon and Nick and I, dressed as neatly as our formal traveling clothes would allow, walked down the street and around the corner and over a couple of utilidors to Dr. Lobart's residence, and into one fine party. At once we met Mrs. Lobart, a charming person of French descent. As I admired her hostess costume—a handsome floor-length skirt of handwoven fabric topped by a simple London wrap accompanied by just-right accessories—I felt the first little twinge of a feeling which said that maybe, just maybe, I would be ready to get back in the world of bright lights by September first. We met her friend, Kay, only arrived that afternoon from New York, with her teen-aged son, Peter. We met Elijah Menarik, the manager of CHAK radio station, a man of Eskimo descent. We met Bertha and Victor Allen, associate editors of the local paper, the *Drum*, and authorities on progress, problems, needs, feelings among the native citizens. (Bertha Allen is of Indian descent, and Victor Allen of Eskimo. This is the kind of intermarriage not yet usual in the Far North, but gradually becoming more so.)

We were served delicious hot hors d'oeuvres, good drink, and excellent conversation. Friends from the Research Laboratory came and went. The young men, Andre, Peter and Devon, sat in the kitchen, strumming on a guitar and singing, providing a pleasant background to all the talk. The *pièce de résistance* was the Eskimo delicacy, muktuk, or whale blubber, flown in that day from the ocean. First Mrs. Lobart served it plain, warmed and cut into tiny pieces as the Eskimos might have done. But, like a true French cook, she also prepared a dish of the bite-sized servings in a marinade of vinegar and her own blend of spices. The room jumped with laughter when Victor, the Eskimo, leaned over to his wife and called,

"There, Bertha! This is how muktuk ought to be served! There! You should find out what she did to it."

And I remember listening in on a conversation between Nick and Dr. Lobart. "You know," the doctor was saying, "there's one more river you might like to try. It's the Thelon, in the Eastern Arctic."

I remember thinking, "The Thelon—never heard of it. There's always one more river, and isn't it wonderful?"

Nick and I left the party around 1:30 a.m. As we walked home we suddenly realized it was dark.

"Look," Nick said, and pointed at the sky.

There we stood, exclaiming over the first stars we had seen all summer.

18 «
REINDEER STATION AND AKLAVIK

Bob Woodland called it "The prettiest Sunday we've had all summer" as we sat over a late breakfast and pulled ourselves together for the boat ride to Reindeer Station. Julie Woodland had the most complicated of tasks: getting two pre-schoolers, and an infant ready for a full day's outing. The rest of us collected anything we could think of for a good picnic on the scow.

A Yukon scow is really a unique flat-bottomed riverboat of extremely shallow draft, powered by an outboard motor, especially designed to meet the needs of transport with a minimum of expense and a maximum of safety and cargo-carrying capacity. Duc's scow was a forty-footer, measuring about three feet wide at the stern, flaring to four feet, then narrowing again at the bow. The first six feet were decked over with marine ply, and the flat bottom of the boat raked upward so that the bow met the waves with the bottom and the whole boat planed the water when loaded properly, even at low speeds. The next eight feet were covered by a tiny plywood cabin. At its front was a hinged window which could be raised or lowered as the weather demanded. The rear of the cabin could be closed by a canvas drop curtain which, when not in use, was rolled and tied to the roof. A foot-wide shelf for maps and compass was just below the window. The steering controls were hooked up to an old automobile steering wheel. A cut-down kitchen chair provided the seat in front of this console. Clutch and speed levers were at the right. The bottom of the boat had duckboards — a wooden scow always seeps a little, if indeed it doesn't downright leak. The sides of the boat were perhaps two feet high; it was painted white, and had no name. This was the boat that

171

could easily and safely carry the ten of us to Reindeer. We were under way by eleven for a glorious two-hour run.

Duc took the wheel of his boat with obvious pleasure. Nick and Dev sat beside him in the tiny cabin, following the channel on the map and the rest of us strung out along the back of the boat among the food boxes and gasoline tins. Fritz and Emma in their faster speedboat would follow and overtake us later. The surface of the water was smooth as silk, the air like summer. Autumn color, even surpassing fall in New England, went mad along the banks. About two-thirds of the way to Reindeer we passed a large channel branching to the west. This was a crossover to the Oniak Channel, the small boat route to Aklavik, and we were told to keep it in mind for our Aklavik trip. Although small trees grew along the edge of the waterways we were now in the region of the Caribou Hills which were covered with Arctic tundra in glorious autumn color. From here on we would be in the true tundra.

Six miles later, after rounding a gentle turn, we could see the station three miles in the distance. Neat and trim and completely captivating, it sat at the base of five-hundred-foot hills amid a stand of dwarfed spruce, willow, and alder. Eskimo children were swimming in the river below the Hudson's Bay store as we approached, but smaller Eskimo children ran to meet us at the dock. When they saw Duc they shouted with pleasure, and swarmed around him. He was their "book man" and they remembered him with affection from his three previous visits.

We walked up the trail from the beach to the boardwalk which is Reindeer Station's Main Street; there is no vehicular traffic. We were expected at the home of Danny and Ruby Sidney — the Woodlands had sent a message by CHAK.

Julie made introductions, and concluded by announcing, "Ruby makes the best coffee in the entire North. When you taste it you will think I serve dishwater at my house."

Pretty flowered china cups and saucers were waiting on the table along with an assortment of cookies. Ruby poured, I tasted, then put down my cup.

"Julie, you are absolutely right! Ruby, this is wonderful!"

Julie told us all, "I took lessons. I had her show me. I used the same measurements, the same amount of water, the same brand of coffee, the same kind of pot. Result: coffee-colored dishwater!"

Ruby suggested a difference in water supply, and we kicked that around for awhile. But I think all three of us women secretly agree that some of us have the gift of making superb coffee, and some of us don't.

Here at Reindeer Station we met Mr. Sven Johannsen, the manager, and learned something of the function of the place. The 'Depot,' as it is also known, is headquarters for the management of the herd of thousands of reindeer which grazes the tundra in a great milling circle a hundred miles across. These animals are treated as domestic animals and raised as we would raise beef, for food. The hides have limited use, and vary in thickness and quality with the season. The summer hides are thin and coarse, a lot like steer hide, and can be tanned so that they do not shed. The winter hides are full and rich and lovely to look at, but they shed anywhere from a little to a lot, no matter how they are prepared. This, of course, makes them of little commercial value, but the reindeer meat is excellent and the annual slaughter is an occasion for festivity. This slaughter, by the way, is not held at the station but is dependent on where the herd has milled to in its tundra grazing. We bought four dried winter hides to have tanned for use as throw rugs.

The herders have their permanent homes and families at the Station. The homes are simple in structure, warm, comfortable, clean. There is a school through grade six for about fifty children. The Women's Institute is an active and meaningful influence in the community.

We walked over to the Hudson's Bay store, which the Factor, of course, opened for us, and here Emma and Nick made a find. One of my husband's hankers was to have a moose hide jacket. Nowhere on the river had we seen anything larger than a vest made from moose. Here at the tiny trading post were a few hides.

Emma said, "You get two hides, and I make your jacket." Nick agreed, and Emma took over.

"You got more hides? These are good ones, but too rough."
The man nodded. "Come with me," he said.

They went through the back of the store, and upstairs to the warehouse. Here from a stack of skins Emma chose two which satisfied her, and the sale was made.

We visited the Aleekuks, and met Mr. Aleekuk. Then we returned to Sidneys' to gather up our families and our belongings.

I still can see Ruby Sidney standing most regally in the living room of her home, and speaking to us with dignity and simplicity:

"You are always welcome in my house," she said, and I felt singularly honored.

On our return trip to Inuvik, Brian rode in the speedboat. He was Emma's boy now. I think she would have kept him for her own, gladly. By the time we reached town the air felt cold although the sky was still fine. Monday we planned our trip to Aklavik, and worried about the weather. Both Duc and Bob thought that Nick and Devon should have more practice with the scow. Also Bob had to lend his kicker to the stranded commercial fisherman, so Duc's 18-horsepower motor had to be installed. Nick and Dev took off for an hour's practice while Emma and I busily ripped the seams on Nick's cloth jacket to use as a pattern for the moose jacket.

The trip across the delta, although only eighty or ninety miles, would take us anywhere from four to eight hours in the slow-moving scow, the time estimate depending on the person to whom we talked. We planned the supplies around two contingencies: 1) everything goes smoothly and we are back next day on schedule; 2) everything fouls up, such as the weather or the motor or our navigation, and we must pull over and sit it out for several days. We packed sleeping bags, minimal cooking and eating gear, all our warm clothes, extra sox, and lots of food. We took our cameras, the first-aid kit, some playing cards, comic books (naturally), and Linc's transistor radio. Nick consulted Bob Woodland, Fritz Feichtinger, and Slim Semmler about the route to take, and all the men agreed on the thinly-pencilled line which threaded the way through the labyrinth of channels: down the East Channel to the Oniak, up the Oniak to the mile-wide Middle Channel, four miles along the Middle Channel to the Napoiak, along the Napoiak to the Schooner Channel, many miles of the Schooner to the Aklavik Channel, then a few miles to where Aklavik is located at the junction of the Peel Channel and the West Channel. It was every bit as complex a navigational exercise as it sounds. Quoting a government-printed tourist guide: "In reaching Aklavik no difficulty should be experienced if the proper channels shown on the map are followed. The whole of the delta, however, is a maze of channels and the canoeist must be careful to follow the channel marked on the chart in reaching Aklavik, otherwise he may find himself wandering for days until he meets someone who can put him on the proper course." All of our friends cheered and encouraged us with such remarks as, "You can't get into too much trouble if you get lost . . . if you run out of gas . . . if you get caught on a sandbar . . . if the first winter storm catches you. Just hole up and someone will come along in a few days to find you."

We met one man who "knew the channels like the palm of his hand" and who one day had arrived five hours late with the basketball team he was carrying to a tournament because he took the wrong turn. We met another who had run his boat so tightly aground on a hidden sandbar that a helicopter had to come and pull him off. We got the impression that no one really believed we would make the trip without mishap, but they all figured the mishaps would not be too catastrophic so why not let us try it.

At last all our gear was safely stowed under a huge waterproof tarp. Forty-five imperial gallons of gasoline were loaded aboard — there are no boatels in the delta. Under the foredecking was a five-horse emergency kicker. Each adult carried three extra shear pins. We said our goodbyes to our friends, promised to phone next morning from Aklavik, and at 1:00 in the afternoon of Tuesday, August 23rd, shoved off from the shores of Inuvik and headed downstream. Nick was at the wheel of the boat. Devon crouched at the rear by the kicker to release the motor lock as the boat finished backing. Brian and

Linc sat by the supplies, ready to start making the lunch. I sat on the decking in front of the cabin and coiled the big painter by which we had been tied to shore.

I think the same sensation hit all of us in the same instant: we were a family again, a team again, responsible only to one another. No longer need we adapt our comings and goings to friends or to a community. No more was there need for company manners. We were free to be ourselves, interrelating according to our real personalities. For just a moment it was pure Distillate of Togetherness, untouched by sentiment, and overwhelmingly joyful.

A few miles down the river we understood how one might come to love traveling like this. Of course we had to raise our voices a bit to make ourselves heard, but there was a lot to be said for watching the river banks glide by as our little kicker hummed along, exerting no more work than a little pressure on the steering wheel. Obviously we had had enough kayaking for one summer. Also the moment we were waterborne something happened to our appetites: we ate more or less constantly all the way to Aklavik.

It became apparent fairly soon that we would be traveling closer to eight hours rather than four, but this was sheer pleasant news for all of us. We traded off on steering, giving Lincoln and Brian their hitches at the wheel too. At all times either Dev or Nick sat at the side of the driver and followed the stream on the map, curve by curve. We were startled when we came to the Middle Channel, for it had been well over a week since we had been on the main river and in that time our memory of the vastness of the Mackenzie had started to fade. But the water was only slightly rumply, our boat moved easily along, and in about twenty minutes we were crossing into the mouth of the Napoiak, having now completed about half of our journey.

Now in this last week of August night was back again as a part of the cycle of days instead of the twilight or 24-hour daylight we had enjoyed so long. We reached Aklavik just as the last light was fading, between 9:00 and 10:00 p.m. and it was drizzling. The banks above the beach looked inviting, but

The Aklavik Temple, Church of England, holds services in three languages — Eskimo, Indian, and English. It is known throughout the Delta for its altar painting: a Nativity with the setting and characters of the Arctic.

Nick stands in the background sporting a carefully barbered 10-week beard. Front, left to right, are the author, Ida Aleekuk, Ruby Sidney, and Julie Woodland, pictured at Reindeer Depot, far above the Arctic Circle.

Along the main street of Aklavik, Devon and Lincoln pose in their new furs. Devon's sheared beaver cap is like those the Mounties wear in winter. Lincoln wears mitts made of bobcat.

New dress styles and old are seen at Inuvik during late summer, however during winter the old will prevail. The Eskimo women at the right have footwear of duffel mukluks covered by rubbers for the street. Their parkas are of muskrat, worn fur-side in, trimmed at the bottom in wolverine. The parka hoods have wide ruffs of wolf, giving rise to the Eskimo name of "sun people" because of its appearance around the face. The gingham Mother Hubbard testifies to early missionary influence.

The grave of the Mad Trapper, fabled in Northwest song and story, stands un-named save for initials near the main street of Aklavik. He murdered several people, including his wife, and was finally brought to bay in true Mountie "we always get our man" fashion in a shoot-out over by Old Crow in the Yukon. The log structure on the left is a cache.

In the Delta we camp on the mud banks. Just beyond the large tent and the fallen tree were the freshest sets of bear tracks we had ever seen.

the town appeared to be asleep. Quickly we made the scow fast, unloaded, and set up our camp near a group of abandoned boats high on the banks. Exploring the town could wait until morning.

In the government pamphlets, Aklavik which means in Eskimo "Place of the Brown Bear," is often referred to as "the historic settlement of Aklavik." The phrase should almost be hyphenated and made a part of the name, it is used so frequently. In fact, when viewed in some lights, it is of some historical significance that Aklavik is still in existence at all. It has always been a busy place, important to both Indian and Eskimo in their fur trading. But about ten to fifteen years ago people became increasingly aware of its limitations insofar as continued growth and progress were concerned for the town is built on unstable land. There is no area nearby for a good all-year airport, nor any room for the town to expand. The idea was put forward to move the town to a better location. Much study and many surveys were made, then several sites were proposed. The site selected for the "New Aklavik" was Inuvik, and the move was under way by 1955. Buildings were dismantled and shipped by barge to the new town. Aklavik, which once had the school, hospital, airport, and administration facilities for the delta found them all transferred to "the world's first truly modern Arctic town."

But in the six years of building the new town more and more of Aklavik's residents thought less and less of moving eighty miles clear across the delta. Came the time for them to move and the reply was "thanks but no thanks."

I don't know when "Proposed new site for Aklavik" and "New townsite of Aklavik" gave way to "Inuvik" but in the 1958 edition of the *Great Slave Lake and Mackenzie River Pilot,* and in all our navigational charts, the new name had not yet been bestowed. Now it seems that people recognize there is room, even need, for both settlements, and Aklavik, far from shriveling into a ghost town, is having a building boom. This was the town we would explore on that rainy Wednesday morning.

Nick and I awoke first, around 7:30, dressed quickly and left the tent without disturbing the others. As we reached the graveled street that paralleled the waterfront, a Northern Affairs and National Resources pickup truck stopped beside us.

"Good morning," Nick said to the driver. "Can you tell us where the restaurant is?"

"It's probably not open yet," he answered. "Come along with us to the office and have a cup of coffee while you're waiting."

A gentle rain was falling. We needed no second invitation. In a few moments we were following our hosts, Rudy Tornow and Carl Larsen, to the quarters above the N.A.&N.R. offices.

"How did you come to town?" asked Tornow.

"In the white scow. Ours is the tent on the beach. We came over yesterday from Inuvik," Nick replied.

"The rest of the family is sleeping," I added.

"You must be the family from the States!"

"Yes."

"How do you find the North?"

The four of us could have talked all morning.

A half-hour later, after coffee, toast, and canned fruit, we left with Rudy for a quick tour of the town. First, however, Nick phoned across the delta to Bob, telling him of our safe arrival and our plans to leave during the noon hour today. In another half an hour we got the general layout of the town, including a stop at the experimental tannery, which was a government project intended to teach the natives the skills necessary in commercial tanning processes. At the time we visited we saw vats filled with muskrat pelts, great drying wheels rotating the skins as they emerged from their chemical baths, and a room where skins were scraped and cleaned. We also saw samples of the finished pelts, and they looked and felt very good to us. At present the tannery is inoperative, and the experiment is being evaluated to see whether or not the North is ready to process its own furs.

Our last stop was at the town water supply, a rather primitive but effective arrangement by which water was piped throughout the town. This was strictly a summertime service, however. During the winter the residents had to keep their own water supply in indoor reservoirs and get much of it by melting ice. While Rudy was explaining the operation of the summer distribution he noticed that one of the pressure gauges registered zero.

"That means trouble," he said. "I've got to get someone on this."

He dropped us off at our tent, first pointing out the restaurant, and went on his way.

With Devon and the boys we went to breakfast, then walked around the town. We saw the community ice house and gazed at the grave of the "Mad Trapper." We looked at the large schoolhouse, sagging pitifully on its pilings, a victim of Aklavik's relentless mire, and now condemned as unsafe. We saw clotheslines in one yard flying a half-dozen patchwork quilts from one line and two drying bear hides from another. We noticed a tiny little weatherbeaten cabin and clutched each other and pointed when we saw a sign still stenciled on its side: CANOL.

Our prime objective was the Aklavik Fur Garment Cooperative and when we finally got inside, again we were transported by the lovely fur garments. Slippers, boots, hats, handbags, mitts, coats, parkas, pillows, wall hangings—we could gladly have walked away with "Some of each, thank you." The variety of furs was impressive too and included wolverine, muskrat, fisher, beaver, bobcat, wolf, and coyote. We were particularly impressed by the fisher — in my opinion, it far surpasses mink. The co-op in Inuvik is one of the outlets for their fur garments; my new muskrat parka had been made there. We spent over an hour, talking to the manager, Mr. Fred Greenland, and coming away with a half-dozen purchases and unfulfilled wishes for a dozen more.

Our last stop before leaving Aklavik was the Episcopal church. The building was plain lapped board, not a bit prepossessing, painted a pale yellow. The sign at the door named the church the Aklavik Temple, and announced that services were held in three lauguages: English, Loucheaux (Indian) and Eskimo. We entered the sanctuary still wondering why people at Inuvik had told us not to miss it.

The moment we entered, we had our answer: the painting over the altar — a nativity for the Far North. Mary was standing with the infant Jesus beside her. Both had Eskimo features, and were clad in white fur parkas and mukluks. Joseph knelt to one side, also a native in Arctic garb. At the other side stood the Magi, but these were not Kaspar, Melchior, and Balthazar, the kings of old. They were, rather, three white traders. Their gifts were pelts and one carried what appeared to be a baby seal. There were no donkey or cattle by the manger, instead the scene was watched by reindeer.

On leaving the church we took to the river in exuberant spirits. Soon we were zooming along at our top ten miles per hour. Before we were even settled, the sound of the motor suddenly changed from its purr to a growly, straining snarl.

Nick shouted, "What's up?"

Dev hollered, "We're aground!"

Nick cut the motor. Quickly I reached down along the side of the scow, pulled out an old oar, and handed it to Devon. Dev thrust the oar into the water, found the channel bottom, and shoved. We all held our breaths.

Reluctantly at first, then easily, the boat started to move. Poling skillfully Devon soon had us afloat. For the second time Nick started the motor and we were off, but rather nicely cut down to size. We hoped that this would be our last hangup. We also hoped that the weather would brighten, that the mild and intermittent rain would soon be over and the day turn mellow again. But as we made our way along the Schooner Channel the air grew colder, and soon we had on all our warmest clothes. The men were busy negotiating the devious passage of the way back, steering so as always to be in the deepest part of the channel, checking carefully each turn in the river with the turns on the map.

Bob had advised us before leaving, "Take a look over your shoulder every now and then at the set of the land behind you. It will all look different when you face it coming back."

This is an old hiking trick, and we had used it often in our backpacking days, but in our river touring, since we followed the current, we had lost the habit. Indeed, we would never have thought of it had it not been for Bob's suggestion. Now the channel going home did not seem completely unfamiliar as it unfolded in reverse.

About the time we re-entered the Napoiak we felt the first threat of wind. Brian and Lincoln and I, riding in the open toward the rear of the boat, took two sleeping bags from the knapsacks, zipped them together, then climbed inside. Down among the rest of our camping gear with the heavy tarp to protect us from rain, spray, and wind we were completely comfortable. We munched crackers and candy bars and watched the scenery roll by.

Gradually, however, the weather grew worse and the ceiling of cloud dropped lower. Wisps of fog rose here and there along the banks. A chop developed on the water surface and as we neared the entrance to the main channel this changed to a definite swell. Now the low ceiling hung more and more like fog, and our view ahead was obscured.

What would be waiting for us in the mile-wide Middle Channel? How hard was the wind blowing, how high the waves?

We remembered the words of the government information sheet: "This is one of the most dangerous stretches of the Mackenzie River because it is open to the winds from the north which are frequent and cause bad traveling conditions. Even the larger river steamers tie up to wait for favorable weather."

If a large boat had no chance in a bad wind there was no chance for us. How hard was the wind blowing? How dense was the fog? If we could not see the opposite shore, how could we risk a crossing? How long could we delay making a decision? Should we take a campsite here in the shelter of the Napoiak? Or could we ease along the west side of the Middle Channel, appraise the situation, and make a landing if the crossing were impossible.

Lying warm and comfortable under the tarp, I chatted now and then with the boys and tried not to think of these decisions that I knew would have to be made.

"Let the men make them," I thought. "They don't need my worries."

The rolling water now had deep troughs and a promise of whitecaps. The fog hung just a few feet above the water's surface. It seemed to me that we must surely be planning to stop. I sat up in the sleeping bag and scanned the near bank for a likely campsite, for firewood, for a protected shelter. I reviewed the menu for a warm dinner. Lincoln, lulled by the cold wind and the boat's movement, had dropped off to sleep.

But little by little the banks fell away, getting further apart, at last disappearing completely. We were entering the main channel — we were not going to stop after all. We turned left, to the north, and I could see the west shore.

"Perhaps we are not really crossing over," I thought hopefully. "Maybe we are going to stop where we can see the main channel and watch for a break in the storm."

But the boat kept on. In ten minutes we passed so many possible stopping places that I knew I was only wishfully thinking.

Then Devon pushed aside the canvas curtain and came out of the cabin. He stood gazing over the top of the shelter, through the mist, toward the east. He stuck his head into the cabin and said something to Nick, then stood up and looked again to the east.

I permitted myself one question.

"Are we crossing?" I asked.

"Yes," Devon answered.

At that moment Nick turned the boat and we headed out into the river, slicing diagonally through the ever-mounting waves.

"I can see the other shore, Mom," Devon added, "It's O.K."

The motor purred, but the wind grew, the waves surged higher and higher, throwing spray back along the sides and spattering it over our tarpaulin. Twice the boat pounded violently as we ploughed into an extra-large comber. I thought of seams parting in the wooden hull, and firmly thrust the thought away as Linc murmured drowsily, "Where are we, Mom?"

"Crossing the main channel, Son. We're almost there."

"Halfway to home," he said, and curled up for sleep again.

I glanced at this confident, trusting boy and felt a cold surge of terror as for a moment I imagined a break in the smooth tone of the motor, a broaching, and a swamped floundering scow in the midst of this menacing river. I thrust that thought away too.

"Fret not thyself," I murmured, and tucked the tarpaulin more snugly about us all. Brian, keeping watch with me, whispered, "This is fun!"

"Yes, isn't it?" I answered too quickly.

Now I looked at Devon whose gaze never wavered from scanning the approaching shore. He watched intently for the cabin landmark that meant the tiny fifty-yard opening to the Oniak Channel and safety. I thought of going to help him, and had even started the move to climb out of the sleeping bag, but some undefined thought stopped me. The boat pounded on.

Suddenly Devon reached down and pulled up the canvas door of the cabin, tying it firmly out of the way so that he could call more easily to his father at the wheel inside. I could see Nick crouched tensely at the little console, his head turned to one side so that he could better hear his son.

Comprehension flooded over me: Nick was steering blind. The water surging over the bow of the boat was completely cutting off his vision!

"Steady as she goes!" Dev shouted.

I looked along the now swiftly-nearing shore. At once I saw the landmark we were watching for: the cabin on the left side of the Oniak. But the cabin was passing by. We had missed the turning. We could not make it!

"Perhaps we are going into a lee by the bank," I thought.

But there was no lee! The waves grew fiercer. From my place in the bottom of the boat I could see their whitecaps breaking well above the sides of the scow. Wilder and wilder they tossed as the full sweep of the north wind bore down on us.

"Ready, Dad!" Devon called.

I looked at Nick. He seemed frozen to the wheel.

"Now!" Dev shouted, leaning into the cabin, then standing erect, the captain of his ship. With a firm grip, Nick spun the wheel to the right. The faithful little motor never faltered. The big scow planed over like a speedboat, her careening sides deflecting the now impotent waves, and executed a beautiful turn of almost a hundred and eighty degrees. We were heading directly into the mouth of the Oniak, the wind and waves now following, helping us on our way.

Just barely was I able to hear Nick saying, "Stand by to come about."

I looked up to see Captain Walter Devon Mitty grinning down at me, exuding self-confidence from every pore of his bearded rain-soaked face. He ducked into the cabin, and flipped down the canvas door.

✦   ✦   ✦

Devon planned to sleep in the boat that night, acting as night watchman over our supplies. Much of our talk that day and the previous one had been of getting an early start to Tuk the next morning. We did not want to impose on Bob and Julie for unloading the boat, the storm having delayed our estimated time of arrival over an hour. But as we turned the scow in toward the beach, and looked with tired relief at our journey's end, there coming down the road from town were Julie's car followed by Bob's truck: they had kept watch for us. We all slept at home.

That night when we were alone Nick said to me, "We can't take the scow to Tuk, Dear. Today's trip convinced me it's too great a risk."

"Yes," I said.

"Let's charter a plane," he went on. "We're too late for a round trip on the sked, but we can get a charter."

"O.K." I said.

"Let's cancel our reservations at the Macdonald and sleep on the couches in the International Airport Tuesday night."

"Fine by me," I said.

"You know, Dear," he continued, "I think summer and even autumn is over. I think winter really started up here today."

But I wasn't paying much attention. I was thinking of summers past, when "Father and Mother" had been the team to guide the family through its adventures. Today it had been "Father and Son" with son giving the orders. I fell asleep while drifting along this branching stream of consciousness.

19 «
TUKTOYAKTUK

Emma and I had work to do: woman's work. There were about twelve more hours of tailoring on the jacket, and there was a three-bedroom apartment to clean. In our eight days at Inuvik, little by little Emma and I became friends. Our family had dinner with the Woodlands but breakfast with the Feichtingers. More accurately, Emma and I had breakfast together after Fritz left for work and long before my sleepy-headed men and boys awakened. Over the coffee cups we exchanged bits of autobiography. Emma's home was Tuktoyaktuk, her birthplace nearby. Her mother, brother, sister, and friends all lived at Tuk and her dream was to return. After a year of living in town, Fritz had had enough of his six-day week, eight to twelve hours a day job at the government garage. He wanted to live "the free life," as he called it.

He had a snow plane—an enclosed cabin on ski runners shoved along by an airplane propeller in the fashion of an Everglades swamp buggy—a cabin in Tuk, a sled, and a dog team. His plan was to set up a winter fish camp far out on the ice pack, about sixty miles from Tuk, and try a commercial fishing venture. Emma, who could neither read nor write, was skilled in the use of modern tools and methods of fur garment making, having learned at the fur co-op in Tuk. She had her own electric sewing machine and her own electric leather welting machine. She regularly produced ook-pik dolls and slippers of Arctic Hare. She worked in sealskin. Her stroud embroidery and bead work were beautiful, and she had an outlet for their sale at the Inuvik Bay. Together they were going back to the more traditional Eskimo way of life for at least a year. Moving day for them was on or about August 30th, the same day we were to leave for the States.

186

Our friends the Woodlands were moving too, but not until December. Bob, who was chief of the N.A.&N.R. garage, had been recommended for a more responsible job in Fort Smith, a small city south of the Great Slave Lake. We reflected on the fact that were we to visit Inuvik in some future year we would again come almost as strangers.

In the late afternoon Nick and I were at the waterfront on an errand which took us to the place where we had beached the scow. Right next to it, pulled well up on the bank, was a traditional 16-foot canoe with a mast for a sail.

"I wonder who's come paddling down the river now," I said.

"No doubt we'll meet them," Nick answered, "News travels fast in this town."

He was right. When we got to the Woodlands for dinner, there in the living room talking to Duc, ever the peripatetic reporter, were Thomy and Virginia Nilsson, a young couple from Edmonton, who had paddled and sailed their rented Hudson's Bay Canoe from Fort Providence. Julie was already reaching for the extra plates as Bob was urging, "Of course you'll stay for dinner."

These two (whom Julie called "the newlyweds" although they assured us they had been married "A long, long time — almost two years") were graduate students at the University in Edmonton. The urge for a change of scene drove them to try the Mackenzie, and now they were confirmed river rats. They planned to get out to Tuk also, somehow, but no real deadline hung over them so they could well wait for "something to come along."

Nick and our family could not wait, however, so during the day he had arranged for a charter. To our mutual satisfaction he had been able to get a floatplane called an Otter (or was it a Beaver?) which carried eight passengers and the pilot. This meant that we could take Bob, Julie, and Duc along as our guests — a small return for their marvelous hospitality.

Julie had never been to Tuk although she and Bob had lived in Inuvik for two years. Just as some people make their first visit to San Francisco's Fisherman's Wharf or Chinatown when

friends from "back East" come to visit, so Julie looked forward
to her first sight of Tuktoyaktuk. Bob was to be the tour guide,
having flown out there once on a repair job for N.A.&N.R.
Again it sounded just like home. Duc, who had been to Tuk
on each of his three previous visits, sat quietly and smiled and
allowed himself to be included in the plans. The charter day
was Saturday, the plane to leave at 11:00 a.m. Bob was to have
his long-promised Saturday off, and Julie arranged for child
care.

Next day, Friday, sped by: time seemed to accelerate. This
was the day that Nick and Dev found a prize souvenir to bring
home: a dried Barrens grizzly bear hide, purchased from Slim
Semmler, the free trader. The men bought it along with two
seal skins. That evening the Woodlands took us to visit with
some special friends of theirs: Slim and Agnes Semmler. We
were delighted to be on the same side of the counter now as
acquaintances rather than as customers.

The Semmlers, like many other people we met and talked
with, are true Northerners, having lived all of their adult years
in this land. They have children and grandchildren, citizens
of the North too. Their loyalty to the Arctic and their superb
confidence that this is the only place in the world to live is
admirable. Like the other couples we met who impressed us
as exemplifying the best qualities of citizenship, these people
are not afraid of work. And if they seem to know the value of
a dollar, they invariably give full measure for every dollar
received.

Before we went to bed that night we phoned from Woodlands' about the next day's charter.

"No need to worry," Nick was told. "Although the plane is
not at Inuvik tonight it will be along in the morning."

"Where is it now?" he asked.

"We had to send it over to Dawson City in the Yukon. It
was supposed to be back tonight, but since it has not come in
yet, we expect it in the morning."

Nick relayed all this to me as we walked home. I had a
qualm or two, but that could wait until tomorrow. We all

turned in, gabbing eagerly about the trip-to-be. I was so excited I could hardly sleep.

By 9:30 a.m. Saturday we were back at Bob and Julie's. The weather was bright, warm, and clear. Nick was proudly wearing the fringed moose jacket which Emma had completed the night before and I wore my new muskrat parka. The boys made do with their sweatshirts from home but were looking forward to buying sweaters with "Tuktoyaktuk" emblazoned on the front. Devon was keeping his fingers crossed that here, in the last town on the edge of the continent, he could find his sealskin jacket.

Nick picked up the phone, dialed the air company, and asked the question. His face sobered, he put down the phone, and turned to the family.

"The plane is not in. They think now it won't be in until Monday."

"What's wrong?"

"They don't know. Either it's weathered in, or has broken down."

"Well, why don't they know? Why don't they phone or radio and find out?"

Now we received another lesson in communications in the Arctic. Although planned, the phone lines across the mountains to the Yukon Territory are not yet installed. These same mountains make direct communication by radio impossible. The Inuvik end of the air charter keeps in touch with its planes by the simple process of deduction: as soon as a plane from Dawson City is airborne and has gained enough altitude for its radio to send from a position above the mountain range, it does so. Therefore, the Inuvik port knows that if it does not hear from a plane that plane is, ipso facto, still on the ground. What is keeping it there is beside the point: grounded is grounded, so why sweat it? We also learned that in a really dire emergency, air contact could be made by a series of relays from Inuvik to Edmonton to Amarillo, Texas, then back up the other sides of the mountains to White Horse, then Dawson City. Obviously our charter could not fall in this category. Besides the plane would surely be here Monday, and we could fly out then—contingent on the weather, of course.

"Why oh why hadn't we taken the sked when we first got into town?" we asked ourselves in vain. But we knew the answers: We wanted first to rest—we were hopeful of getting a ride with the Research Institute—we thought we could go out on a commercial fishing trip—we thought the government barge was available—we planned on the scow—and so tomorrow, and tomorrow, and tomorrow.

For the next two hours Nick and Bob phoned everywhere to arrange an alternate charter but nothing was available. Business had never been so good or planes so broken: All available transport seemed either to be "out of order" or "in the air."

"Don't worry," our friends tried to console us, "There's not much out there to see anyway."

But we had come on purpose, to see for ourselves, and we were mighty depressed.

Then the phone rang, and Nick was on the line.

"A plane for four? But we are five. Two are just young boys. Their combined weight is like one adult. I'll call you back."

Nick hung up, then gave us the news.

"The word has gotten around. There is a small plane, but it can only take four, adults or children. There are regulations about safety belts."

Immediately Duc and Julie and Bob said "forget about us."

Duc, who was staying another five or six weeks, said, "I'll go out on the sked in September."

Bob reminded us, "We can drive out there on the river in a car when it's frozen over," even though they never had and probably never would.

"So it's up to you five to decide," Julie concluded.

There we sat and looked around at one another.

One of the features of the summer had been the "all for one, one for all spirit," something of a rarity in our back-home life. Except for the trip to Canol we had shared every adventure. During our stay at Inuvik a few chances had come our way for one of us to ride along to different places on a charter, but we had always turned them down in the hope that we could all go later together. Now that we were down to the wire, one of us would have to stay.

The air was tense with indecision. To dream so long of standing on the shore of the Arctic! To be so close to reaching the goal! Seventy miles—45 minutes by air!

I have the impression that each of us was preparing to make the offer when Brian spoke up.

"I'll stay," he announced firmly.

We all turned to him.

"Brian!" Linc exclaimed, "Oh, Brian, No!"

"Yes," he answered. "It's O.K. I'll stay—I've decided." Then he turned away from us and walked out of the room.

We all sat quiet for a moment. Then we moved.

"Come on! Let's go! Call the air company! We'll bring Brian something nice!"

Amidst the hubbub we pulled ourselves together and scurried down to the dock. There in the water was a little Cessna floatplane. The pilot, yawning sleepily, was ready. In moments we were aboard, and as we strapped ourselves in I remember waving to Brian, who stood smiling bravely on the wharf. I don't think he appreciated the manliness of what he did, but I do and I shall never forget it.

Airborne in the smoothest of take-offs we were soon curving out over the town which lay, doll-house size below us. We could see at a glance its orderly plan. The silvery aluminum structures housing the utility pipes wove their shiny pattern all over one-half the town, tying the homes together in a sort of Mondrian. In a few minutes the town was behind us and we flew straight out over the Arctic Barrens, the true tundra, on our way to the Beaufort Sea. Now we observed the phenomenon called "polyganization," a patterning in the land below which makes this peculiar design. The number of lakes astonished us—there must have been hundreds—some connected by channels, some merely puddles standing all alone. Next to the blue water stunted willows grew, but all else was overgrown with the low scrubby cover of the tundra, and the multicolored patterns of lichen: bronze, red, orange, yellow, brown, green. I tried to imprint it on my mind.

A half-hour out of Inuvik we neared our first pingo, and again we were agog with excitement. A pingo is a mountain of ice which has erupted from a subterranean fresh water lake. In appearance it is like a volcano. The top is split as though lava had once poured out, and the sides are covered with tundra. But beneath the thin layer of lichen and dirt lies solid blue ice. These pingoes are many years old and several hundred feet high. Rising from the flat frozen plains they look immense. Several guard the entrance to Tuk, the only place in the world where they are found. Why they form is still a mystery.

Next we came in sight of the radar dome of the DEW line, and a few minutes later we landed in a slight chop on the water of a little cove, the edge of the true Arctic Sea, and taxied to the floating wharf. We were in Tuktoyaktuk.

Original plans had been for us to stay five days here. Now we had two hours. As we stepped out of the plane the pilot cautioned us, "Keep one eye on that fog bank out there."

We looked where he was pointing. Only a few miles north we could see great blotches of fog reaching to the horizon.

"If that bank starts to move, run for the plane. This place can get so socked in in five minutes that we'd never get out of here!"

With that he curled up on the back seat for a nap while we toured the town.

The first stop was the fur co-op, and Devon's Great Moment was at hand. For a thousand miles we had heard, "I just want a sealskin jacket."

Now he asked the clerk, "Do you have any parkas in sealskin?"

The answer was immediate, "No, sorry, no sealskin parkys."

Devon's erect posture drooped. He shrugged slightly, and turned away.

The clerk continued, "But I do have one sealskin jacket."

"Jacket?" Dev repeated, "I mean jacket!"

"Yes, here on the rack. Would you like to try it?"

This is a pingo, a mountain of ice, covered with a thin layer of tundra, and rising between 150 and 200 feet elevation. There are many of these strange formations surrounding Tuktoyaktuk, the only place in the world where they are found.

The tundra, the Arctic desert, from the bush plane on the way to Tuktoyaktuk. Lakes, some isolated, some connected by channels, form in every depression of the land and look to be countless.

In the background of the floatplanes' lagoon are two of Tuk's three churches. The power lines supply the DEW line station located nearby. July is the one month Tuk can hope to have little fog; in August the town can almost vanish within five minutes if the fog starts rolling in.

Tuktoyaktuk from the air, with view over the Arctic Ocean. Here, we were told, the sea is too far north to show appreciable tide changes.

Standing on the tundra, at the northernmost edge of continental North America, Lincoln gazes far out across the Beaufort Sea of the Arctic Ocean. At the skyline lies the perpetual ice pack. Only a few days after this picture was taken the water started its winter freezing to begin again the annual ice bridge to the polar pack.

Devon emerges in triumph from the floatplane which carried him to Tuk-Tuk, wearing the sealskin jacket he found at the edge of the continent. His packages contain fur garments of Arctic hare and muskrat, gifts for friends back home.

Richard Nickerson, leader and photographer of the expedition, stands by three bales of dried hides — reindeer, seal, and grizzly bear — obtained in local trade. He also wears the fringed moose jacket made for him by an Eskimo friend.

In an instant Devon was out of his traveling jacket and into the sealskin, which fit as if it had been tailored for him. He was speechless at first. He stood in front of a mirror and stared and stroked the sleek fur. The tailor had done a superb job, cutting and matching the perfect figured skins of the Sachs Harbour Arctic Hair Seals. After catching his breath, Devon asked, "How much?"

The clerk named the price.

"Wrap it up," said Nick.

"Wrap me up with it then," Devon quipped. "I'm never going to take it off!"

Next stop was the Bay, for mail and in the last hope of finding some soapstone carving. Both mail and soapstone were there. Our family and friends were certain we would get to Tuk, so they had written. And at last we viewed a collection of excellent carvings for sale. We bought a figure of an Eskimo woman and child for a friend back home, and a particularly nice little carved otter for Brian. Then we split and went our separate ways around the town.

Besides the Bay and the fur shop, Tuktoyaktuk has three missions: Roman Catholic, Anglican, and Evangelical. There is a federal day school, a Royal Canadian Mounted Police detachment, a hotel, a cafe, a movie house, and a free trader's store. About fifty Eskimo families live in the settlement. Tuktoyaktuk, usually called "Tuk" or "Tuk Tuk" in the North, was permanently settled in 1934 as a Hudson's Bay trading post. The name means "Resembling a Caribou" and is the Eskimo name for the spot that was officially named "Port Brabant." Old maps identify Tuk as Port Brabant, but the local usage won over and the name was officially changed.

The Distant Early Warning Line station employs most of the Eskimo wage earners. Loading and unloading ships, fishing, and trapping are the other sources of revenue for the natives. Sports fishing is available, as are trips on whale and seal hunts, but the tourist must take the initiative in arranging for such ventures. Tourism is more of a dream than a reality.

I met Emma's mother, brother, and sister-in-law while looking around town, and also a cousin and several friends. Nick and Devon and Linc meanwhile explored Tuk's community deepfreeze storage system: rooms hand-hewn out of ground ice, entered by a shaft and tunnel behind the Hudson's Bay store. At last we met again, our two hours almost at an end. We walked to the little cemetery which stands at the edge of the sea, and looked out over the Arctic toward the ice pack which lay just over the horizon. Then we ran for the plane. Just before boarding we saw a sight which Nick immediately photographed.

"See the primitive Eskimo family in their primitive Eskimo kayak," he announced.

There was a man, a woman, and a little child, dressed in fur-trimmed working parkas, wearing mukluks covered by rubbers, hauling up their sleek fiberglassed outboard powered by at least a 35-horsepower Mercury kicker.

"Only crazy American tourists paddle kayaks," Devon said.

In the evening at Inuvik we heard on the CHAK "announcements" that Tuk was totally fogged in.

The Northwest Territories had one more glorious autumn day left to show us: next day, Sunday, August 27. Once more we provisioned the scow, and Duc, the Woodlands, and our family went to Reindeer Station where we visited our Eskimo friends for the last time, then started for home in the late afternoon. By the time we reached Inuvik, clouds covered the sky, the temperature was dropping, and rain was only an hour away.

Monday, our last day, was a day for many chores. Often, now that I am home, I find myself describing how we would "pull over and camp" each night, or "haul in and throw together the tents" when threatened by rain. When people ask how we traveled to and from the river my reply too often is a glib "we just tossed our things on a plane and flew." Forgotten are the long miles of searching for a habitable place to camp; forgotten the rain-soaked clothes when we lost a race against the weather; forgotten the hours of planning, the lists of food and equipment, the mail orders and shopping trips; forgotten the seemingly endless yards of red tape in packing, packaging, labeling, and shipping equipment.

We spent the morning hours packing, securing permits for our animal pelts, arranging surface shipment for our boats and tents, confirming tickets and reservations, and checking baggage. Then we went for a last walk around the town in the rain. Once more we photographed the utilidors, the sturdy aluminum-sheathed surface "tunnels" which carry the water and waste for the government-owned part of town. The main branches are supported on four-foot piles, well above the permanently frozen ground. The housing itself is a four-foot square box-like tunnel, and large wooden stiles, staircases of twelve to fourteen steps, are placed strategically for ease in crossing from yard to yard of the living compounds. Brian and Linc had learned from their friends that the space beneath the utilidors made wonderful long corridors in the snow during winter. In the summer you shun the use of the stiles and "do the limbo" under the utilidors if you must cross over.

We walked through the "re-hab" area where tiny log cabins, government administrated, housed some of the needy. We saw again the "co-op" part of town where privately-built, privately-owned dwellings were being erected at an accelerating pace, but we were never able to learn why it was called the co-op. We walked by the community refrigeration and deepfreeze buildings, so necessary for food preservation all year around, and smiled as we remembered Julie saying, "In mid-winter you walk into the deepfreeze and it feels warm." We noticed again the multiple electrical outlets at the front of each building, where during the winter you actually plug in your car: heating units placed on vital parts of the car keep it operable during the dark cold season. Everywhere we went we heard the sounds of radio CHAK, and we remarked again about the ubiquitous radio. Back home we are awakened each morning by our clock radio, and our first conscious gesture is to turn the thing off. Up here the first daily act in each home is for someone to turn the radio on—loud—and it never gets turned down or off until bedtime.

At last we returned to Feichtingers' where Fritz was working over his snowplane. Nick stayed outdoors to help while I went in to see how Emma was doing.

"How's it going?" I asked.

"All good," she smiled, gesturing at spotless woodwork and sparkling windows. "Last is the floors."

"Let's have a cup of coffee," I suggested, "then I'll help."

We sat down to coffee and doughnuts in the kitchen. Suddenly Fritz burst in, and called out, "Where is the iodine?"

"You hurt?" his wife asked.

"Ja, just a little." He had found the iodine and in the old-fashioned way was about to pour some of the medicine into a freely-bleeding cut.

"I get the Band-aid," Emma said, and reached toward the shelf behind him. In that moment the iodine penetrated the wound, Fritz let out a yelp, and dropped the bottle on the floor. The miserable brown stain splattered everywhere.

"Oh, what do we do?" Emma cried.

"Paper towels," I said, and snatched a wad. "Now do you have scouring pads?"

"Yes, here," she said, and handed me a box of them.

"Now water."

Quickly Emma filled a pail of water. I was on my hands and knees, wiping, rinsing, and scouring briskly. In a few moments Emma saw the floor emerging bright and clean and dropped down beside me to help. Fritz, seeing the situation would be improved by his absence, slipped outside to his work.

Little by little the job was done. Now we were under the kitchen table, working along together on a part of the floor which the iodine had not touched. In place of scouring pads we were using rags, and one of us had added a detergent to the water. I reached over and picked up a small bread crust, tossed it in the direction of the sink, then looked up at Emma who was in the process of picking up a bit of dropped breakfast bacon. At that instant she looked up at me. We started to laugh. On hands and knees, beneath that kitchen table, we laughed and laughed until the tears rolled down our faces. Then we sat back on our heels, bumping our heads on the table in the process, and laughed some more.

"Emma," I gasped when I could speak, "whoever heard of such a thing?"

"We didn't sweep the floor!"

Off into more gales we went. No housewife in the entire world, we laughed, would think of washing a floor without first sweeping.

When we could breathe again we said,

"Oh well, might as well finish." So we did, picking out bits with our fingers, washing, rinsing, drying, and giggling to the total bafflement of Devon and the boys. They, being male, could not be expected to understand this basic truth in the universality of housewifery.

✓   ✓   ✓

Tuesday afternoon, plane time was at hand and we had said our last goodbyes. Duc took us to the airport where the four-motored DC-6 of Pacific Western Airlines was waiting. Nearby stood a two-engined cargo plane loading for a short haul to Tuk. As we watched, a flat-bed truck drove up carrying Fritz and Emma and her beloved sewing machines. A fork lift took the crated machines from the truck bed and deposited them in the plane. My last sight of Emma was as she clambered aboard after them and disappeared in the hold, followed soon by Fritz.

Then our flight was called. We turned to Duc, who was to stay another month at Inuvik.

"So long," he said. "See you fellas later"—the modern Eskimo words of farewell!

We walked across the gravel runway in the lightly falling rain, and although we could not know it at the time, the plane we were boarding was the last one out of Inuvik for the next ten days; the first winter snowstorm moved in that night.

I remember the Arctic as bathed in perpetual light, warm, mild, beautiful with the life of its fleeting summer. Could we have met the challenge of the dark frozen winter months with anything like the eagerness shown by the real dwellers in the North? Sometimes I think that had we missed that plane we would have stayed to see for ourselves.